Dreamers
of
God

by

David Fenton

Dreamers of God
1st Edition July, 2020

Published by Star Label Publishing
P.O. Box 1511, Buderim, QLD, Australia
publishing@starlabel.com.au

ISBN: 978-0-6484602-2-0

To Jesus my Saviour
To Angela my lovely wife
To Lily-Anne my amazing daughter
To my Mum and Dad for believing
and investing!

Contents

ACKNOWLEDGEMENTS

I want to thank all those who have supported me and encouraged me in my journey with Christ Jesus!

To Gateway Ministries for all the years of love and support! To Daryl and Marjorie Reynolds giving me an opportunity to minister starting at age seven in your home group!

I would like to thank Uncle Tom and Aunt Marilou McDonald and all the family for the years of mentoring and input and for being people of faith and grit! I am thankful for a lifetime literally of love and support!

I want to acknowledge the one and only John Paul Jackson who always believed in me and helped me and told me straight, I can't wait to see you again!

I want to thank Dennis and Judy Hughes for all the encouragement calls and prayer and accurate prophetic words spoken to myself and family!

I want to also acknowledge my parents who have always shown nothing is a bother, that you always believed and trusted in Jesus! That you taught me to seek God and His kingdom first! I can never say or express my love and thankfulness enough to you both!

Thank you so much Star Label Publishing for all the encouragement, technical help, advice and for the amazing work that you do!

Lastly, I want to acknowledge my loving wife Angela and daughter Lily-Anne! I could never have done this without your support!

INTRODUCTION

One thing that all humans have in common is the ability to dream. We dream of the past, the present and the future. Dreams of survival, revival, fight and/or flight. We dream in the day and at night; dreams of flying above the ground, into space and beyond, fighting some rough and tough foe, defending our family, triumphing over adversity, searching to find a lost item, a lost love or opportunity, racing to catch a plane, train or other mode of transportation, or giving a moving speech to the world that motivates and elevates us all. These are all dream experiences.

However, the processes and priority by which we place importance on dreams is varied. This variance is a mixture of factors dealing with importance based on a person's personal value, as well as cultural and societal emphasis on the validity and value of dreams. Dreams, however, can remain a major part of a person's life and even become a part of the morning routine. Some people make a habit to write down the contents of their dream in a journal or a dream portfolio. Others diminish their ability to remember dreams by failing to concern themselves, or even think cognitively about dreams or their unconscious thoughts. Others blatantly dismiss dreams as simply being a thought processes—a way to keep the brain's function going while at rest. While some put forth that dreams are stimulated by chemical releases, or a biological function or process, and therefore place no further critical, serious or spiritual weight upon dreams of any kind.

Modern day psychologists such as Freud, Jung, and Perls—as well as others—have offered alternative interpretations of how to deal with dreams. There are also much earlier historical thinkers who tackled, or teased out, ideas around dreams. Ancient texts, such as The Holy Bible, also speak of dreams and encounters with a living God through the use and interpretation of dreams.

Although it's not my intention to write a book on the historical perspectives of dreams, I feel it is important to first have a working knowledge, and some level of understanding of how dreams have been conveyed to the western world. As such, before I introduce you to the 'Dreamers of God' let's take a look at historical, psychological, cultural and Christian perspectives of dreams.

Historical perspectives on Dreams

Western society has largely had a resistance concerning dreams, its study, understanding, and the interpretations through dreams. It is only recently through the nineteenth century that there has been attention given to dreams from a Christian perspective. Using the Bible as a foundational basis, we see three themes appear: the use of dreams; prayer; and angelic encounters. What is interesting here, is that generally, the modern church as a whole—perhaps in some cases for seemingly good reasons—does not acknowledge or engage these themes.

Our Western society has been influenced by philosophers who, though intelligent and articulate, were coming from a reasoned and logical point of view concerning spiritual things. In regard to revelations from God, 1 Corinthians chapter 2 verses 9-16 says:

> But, as it is written, "What no eye has seen, nor ear heard, nor the heart of man imagined, what God has prepared for those who love him"—these things God has revealed to us through the Spirit. For the Spirit searches everything, even the depths of God. For who knows a person's thoughts except the spirit of that person, which is in him? So also no one comprehends the thoughts of God except the Spirit of God. Now we have received not the spirit of the world, but the Spirit who is from God, that we might understand the things freely given us by God. And we impart this in words not taught by human wisdom but taught by the Spirit, interpreting spiritual truths to those who are spiritual.

> The natural person does not accept the things of the Spirit of God, for they are folly to him, and he is not able to understand them because they are spiritually discerned. The spiritual person judges all things but is himself to be judged by no one. "For who has understood the mind of the Lord so as to instruct him?" But we have the mind of Christ.

David Fenton

Psychological perspectives
on Dreams

Psychology, since its foundation in the early 1900's has had a considerable focus on dreams. Psychologists: Sigmund Freud; Carl Jung; and Fritz Perls in particular, given that their work has been taught to many, are worth consideration and discussion in relation to their views on dreams. As such, a brief overview is relevant to review their work and basic beliefs concerning dreams, and to help us understand the currency of dreams in a modern world.

Freud – Dream as 'Interpretation'

Sigmund Freud's *The Interpretation of Dreams*, published in 1900, focuses on the topic of dreams and the unconscious. It is my opinion, that this is an analysis of dreams and not true interpretation of dreams. I say this, because he left little, to no space for any God inspired connotation placed upon or within dreams.[1]

Freud regarded dreams as a royal road to the unconscious, and because of that, dream interpretation has been an important psychoanalytic technique. There were two main factors or keys for his theory. The first was: what are the materials of dreaming? The second is: how do these materials work together? According to Freud, dreams include stimuli from the external world; subjective experiences; organic stimuli within the body of a person; and mental activation during sleep.[2]

Doctor Freud's practical application to the conscious and to dreams was simple. He thought that the unconscious wanted to make itself known through dreams, but the dreamer supressed the attitudes. He believed there was a censor ability within the dreamer; that there are gaps that the dreamer won't even be aware of; and he explained there is a difference between the actual dream and the original dream thought in a dreamer. At the basis of his belief about dreams and the unconscious, is a sexually suppressed wish found from childhood that is stimulated or stirred as we get older.

Doctor Freud also believed that it didn't matter if the client or patient agreed that they felt the interpretation was correct, because the dreamer is not aware of his or her subconscious thoughts and feelings.

This style of interpretation of dreams has been coined with the doctor's surname, 'Freudian'. It is filled with sexual erotic overtones and meanings. The Freudian student would believe that dreams were given to guard or protect a person's sleep.

According to this style of dream analysis, there are four categories that dreams can be placed into to describe what is going on in the life of the dreamer. Condensation, displacement, symbolisation and secondary revision, according to Freud. Condensation is where there is a disguising of two or more thoughts condensed into a single image or idea. The second: displacement, is where the client takes a feeling pertaining to a thought attached to one situation and then displaces it to another, in order to distract the dreamer from true feelings. The third is symbolisation, which is disguising infantile sexual feelings. The fourth and last, is secondary revision, which is taking puzzling material in the mind and attempting to conform it to a person's known expectations.

David Fenton

Jung – Dreams as a Serial Archetype

Carl Jung presents another style of dream analysis. Jungian theory 'is based upon the belief that the unconscious state does not think rationally, but metaphorically and symbolically, and uses images'. Jung wrote a book in 1912 called *The Psychology of the Unconscious*. Unfortunately, he is known for this writing and, it seems, was etched out in the thinking of the Christian circles in a certain way. Jung admitted himself that this publication was, 'sins of my youth'. Jung's writings are not just theory, but based upon experience; and because many people didn't have the experience, the church discounted much of what he was trying to convey.[3]

To try to be as simplistic as possible, this format of analysis was based on the belief that there was an archetype (the masculine and the feminine side of each person). It uses mythology, different religion beliefs and history. Jungian theory looks at dreams as a series and not individually. The dreamer can interpret it whatever way is most comfortable or usable. Jung introduced his study by stating that there are two ways of thinking, analytical and symbolic. He believed that in one way of thinking we are active, and in the other we are passive.[4]

Saul McLeod says in his article on Carl Jung:

> Jung was a supporter of Sigmund Freud, and Freud requested Jung become president of the International Psychoanalytical Association which formed in 1910. However, after publicly criticizing Freud's theory of the Oedipus complex and his emphasis on infantile sexuality in 1912, Freud and Jung split.

Jung, however, continued to develop his own version of psychoanalytic theory. Freud and Jung did agree that there are, what can be called, universal symbols that come out of a person's soul and tell us its very nature and structure. Jung named this 'the collective unconscious.

On the whole modern psychology has not viewed Jung's theory of archetypes kindly. Ernest Jones (Freud's biographer) tells that Jung "descended into a pseudo-philosophy out of which he never emerged" and to many his ideas look more like New Age mystical speculation than a scientific contribution to psychology. [5]

However, according to McLeod,

Jung's work has also contributed to mainstream psychology in at least one significant respect. He was the first to distinguish the two major attitudes or orientations of personality – extroversion and introversion. He also identified four basic functions (thinking, feeling, sensing, and intuiting) which, in a cross-classification, yield eight pure personality types.[5]

Perls – Dreams as an expression of yourself

Fritz Perls believed that "You are the maker of the dream …Whatever you put into the dream must be what is in you."[6]

Perls developed a methodology in regard to dreams called, *Gestalt*. Gestalt holds a holistic view of man, denying the classic belief in mind-body being separated—it seeks to involve the total person to be fully aware of oneself. The parts of a person will include a person's thoughts, behaviours, body, and, most importantly, emotions. The Gestalt theory is about healing the person who is dreaming.

Perls sought to find 'a relaxed perception by the whole person'. The theory is based upon the belief that what is needed for healing neurosis is a living experience in the here and now, with full awareness of oneself. Following this theory, awareness is much more than knowing facts about oneself. Awareness is the ability to be present with oneself in the exact moment; the ability to experience life without 'interrupting' oneself with emotional defence mechanisms.

When applied to dreams, the Gestalt theory attempts to use the dream images as a way to be experiencing the feelings attached to them. Perls agreed with Freud and Jung in that the content of dreams are aspects of the dreamer's own psyche, but instead of attempting to discover the 'hidden content', or the meaning of the images, Gestalt sought to find the effect, or emotion, attached to each dream image. For example, if one dreams of skiing on a slope of snow, Gestalt might ask the patient to 'be the snow' and express how the snow feels in the dream.

The summary of Perls' approach to dreams was not to interpret them, but to see dreams as a way in which a person could start to bring back parts of their life that were missing or perhaps not being experienced or expressed in the emotions of the dreamer.[6]

Since Freud, Jung and Perls, there have been many modern scientists that have submitted different psychological theories regarding dreams. In her article on The Conversation entitled *Was Freud right about dreams after all?* Josie Malinowski says:

> Dozens of theories about why we dream now exist — from helping to process of our emotions and strengthening our new memories to rehearsing social or threatening situations. But no one theory now dominates, as Freud's once did. However, over the past decade or so, a new series of experiments have begun to demonstrate that at least one part of Freud's theory might have been correct after all: that we dream of things we are trying our best to ignore.[7]

Dreams in a Laboratory

The study of dreams in scientific research laboratories really started with the breakthrough discovery of REM sleep, by Aserinsky and Kleitman (1953).[8] These men received the credit for the discovery of "rapid eye movements," which is the characteristic of REM sleep. In her article, *A Brief History of Dream Research*, Dr Michelle Carr expands:

> Around the same time, Calvin Hall was working on a new cognitive theory of dreaming, and in 1966, Hall and Van de Castle created and published a thorough content scoring system for dreams (Hall & van de Castle, 1966).[9]

In an example of recent breakthroughs which came after 1953, neuroimaging of lucid dreams produced neural correlations of dream activity, similar to activity that would be found in wake.

For instance, fMRI BOLD responses were observed in the same sensorimotor cortical regions for both wakefulness and lucid dreaming, though activation during dreaming was weaker and more localized (Dresler et al., 2011).[9]

The world of dreams has become more and more scientifically interesting. Allan Hobson and Robert McCarley presented a model of dreaming called the Activation-Synthesis hypothesis.[10]

There is more and more study on this fascinating subject and new names of interest, as people want to unravel the mystery of dreams. Names like J.A Hobson, M. Jouvet, M, Solms, J. Zhang, M. Carr, and many more names.

It is my opinion, that these theories have moulded the modern-day perception of dreams and the interpretation of dreams. Like most things, there is truth in some of it and, for a consistent explanation of dreams or the interpretation of dreams, I still adhere to the Word of God as my source. I respect people's opinions and I have many friends within the psychology world. I love how many people now describe biblical definition of dreams and understanding of interpretation, as an ancient form of Hebraic dream interpretation, which I would agree there is a lot of merit to in the description and method. I am very glad to see science being used to explore the mystery of dreams. There are several individuals who find it fascinating, giving helpful insight into how we are made by the Creator.

Cultural Perspectives
on Dreams

Through my own walk with Jesus in the area of dreams, I have found there are modern day cultures that do place a value on dreams. The Jewish culture is one of the most ancient cultures, with many examples in the Old Testament to this fact. When I visited Israel in 1999, I was able to discuss this subject with a good number of followers of Judaism, as well as a very welcoming Rabbi, on the subject.

The Aboriginal people of Australia are very open to dreaming as a form of communication with the Creator. I have lived and ministered in Australia for many years now, and have had numerous discussions on the subject of dreams, with tribal elders of different Aboriginal nations.

The Native American Indigenous communities place great value on dreams and visions. I was fortunate enough to learn this first-hand, when I was a young man in my late teens/early twenties, through discussion with people from the great nation of the Iroquois peoples from different tribes and clans. There are nomadic communities in Europe who, also, place a high value on dreaming.

The people from the nation of Papua New Guinea place a high worth on dreams in their culture and I have had several conversations with people from this nation about dreams and the value of dreams.

David Fenton

Christian Perspectives on Dreams

I was amazed to learn in 2006 that, in some cases, churches who actually gathered to pray and worship, would then sleep in the same vicinity to dream, then share what God had spoken through their dream.

> For I have bent Judah as my bow; I have made Ephraim its arrow. I will stir up your sons, O Zion, against your sons, O Greece and wield you like a warrior's sword. (Zachariah chapter 9 verse 13)

This is an interesting Scripture, which I believe is talking about those who would approach things just from the logical and the learned academic format, as opposed to those who would want to see the spiritual journey in Christ and follow the ancient paths of truth.

Methodism

One of the first Western written books on dreams was by a man named David Simpson in 1791 called *Discourse on Dreams and Night Visions*. Simpson was a reported close friend of John Wesley (1703-1791), leader of the revival movement known as Methodism.
Simpson wrote:

> Several of them have been attended with the most important consequences in the history of mankind: and they are all so interwoven with the sacred story, that they cannot be rejected without shaking the credit of the whole book wherein they are found. But the truth

of the Holy Scripture is established upon such and immovable foundation that it can never be subverted, but upon principle that would overturn the faith of all history. Before we can commence infidels, therefore, with respect to these parts of the Bible, which record the divine interpositions by dreams and night-visions, we must be prepared to reject the whole system of revelation. For the credit of the former stands or falls with the latter.[11]

Other early known books on dreams include, Canon Burnett Streeter's, *Reality*, published in 1927 and a Spanish Jesuit priest named Pedro Meseguer published a work called, *The Secret of Dreams*. Still these works are few and far between when compared with other biblical topics.

Aristotle - the Sleep and Waking Approach

Aristotle, a Greek philosopher, maintained that anything not tangible and logical was irrelevant in life. This influenced a lot of cultures who took to the Greek style of learning and approach to life. Interestingly, Aristotle wrote three books on dreams: *On Sleep and Waking; On Dreams;* and *Prophecy in Sleep*. These were ground-breaking concepts, never really thought about or approached before like this, on the subject of dreams.[12] Aristotle's main contention was, that a person was more sensitive and more able to perceive when sleeping. However, he would not attribute any dreams to the gods but, for natural reasons, dreams took place.

Aquinas – the Reasoned Approach

Italian philosopher, Thomas Aquinas (1225-1274), promoted the idea that people can only know truth through reason and the five senses. This is also very interesting as Thomas Aquinas had a vision while writing his book, *Summa Theologica*, toward the end of his life, which he never finished. He had such a disturbing encounter through a dream, in which Peter and Paul instructed him on a theological point he was pondering and having difficulty with for the book, that he quit writing the book. Aquinas said, "I can do no more. Such things have been revealed to me that all I have written seemed like straw, and I now await the end of my life."[13]

Polycarp – The Prophetic Approach

When researching dreams in church history, we see that many church fathers in the early church were open to dreams and visions in the daily life of the believer and their own journey in the faith. Polycarp (AD 69-155) was the Bishop of Smyrna and a disciple of the Apostle John. He dreamed that he would be martyred in Rome. He saw his pillow under his head catch on fire, and he realised that this image of destruction signified his own capture and death.[14]

Origen – Dreams 'The Well of Vision'

Early Christian scholar, ascetic and theologian, Origen of Alexandria (AD 185- 254), believed that dreams were from God. Origen had a debate with a pagan named

Celsus, who was an antagonist of Origen. Celsus made claims ridiculing the dreams that surround the truth of Jesus' birth. Origen responded with this statement:

> "And that in a dream certain persons may have certain things pointed out to them to do, is an event of frequent occurrence to many individuals, —the impression on the mind being produced either by an angel or by some other thing. Where, then, is the absurdity in believing that He who had once become incarnate, should be led also by human guidance to keep out of the way of dangers?" [15]

Irenaeus – Dreams 'Reveal God's Likeness and Nature'

Irenaeus (AD 200), the Bishop of Gaul, believed dreams were a way for him to maintain proper contact with God. He was a minister who fought against gnostic beliefs that were popular with 2nd century intellectuals. Irenaeus believed that dreams were revelations of a spiritual world. He wrote a work called *Against Heresies,*

> and believed that Peter's dream, itself, was proof of the authenticity of the experience (see Acts chapter 10). 'He used the understanding of dreams to refute the belief in reincarnation and transmigration of souls.

He believed that even though,

> God is Himself invisible to the eye directly, he gives us visions and dreams through which he conveys the likeness of his nature and his glory...That God manifests Himself, not only through mighty works,

but through the use of both visual and auditory visions as well.[16]

The early church had amazing minds on its side. One of those individuals was a man name Clement from Alexandria. Clement was raised as a pagan. He was at Alexandria in the 2nd century. Clement stated:

> Let us not, then, who are sons of the pure light, close the door against this light; but turning in on ourselves, illuminating the eyes of the hidden man, and gazing on the truth itself, and receiving its streams, let us clearly and intelligibly reveal such dreams as true.[17]

Artemidorus

A man named Artemidorus of Daldis, who lived in the 2nd century AD, wrote a comprehensive text, *Oneirocritica* (The Interpretation of Dreams). He believed that dreams could predict future events and that also they could include puns. Greek works on dream interpretation, such as Artemidorus, were translated into Arabic. A fourteenth-century copy of his work, containing the first three books, is preserved in Istanbul University.[18]

Modern Day

My point in sharing history is to establish dreams as a foundational truth, one which is not a new subject. As the Bible reminds us in Ecclesiastes chapter 1 verse 9: "What has been is what will be, what has been done is what will be done, and there is nothing new under the sun".

Dreamers of God

We live in a modern world with all sorts of thought, thinking, experiences and explanations. My desire in writing *Dreamers of God* is to draw people back to the Bible as the written Word of God, a thorough, historically documented and amazing standard of writing and the 'living Word of God', that we simply call the Bible. As we take a look through the Scriptures, we will see differences in the reasons and why a person receives a dream. It is my intention to help people see dreams from a godly perspective, being open to consider that a dream can be initiated by God for the purpose of communicating with us.

As we now dive deep into His Word let's remember:

> They said to him, "We have had dreams, and there is no one to interpret them."
> And Joseph said to them, "Do not interpretations belong to God? Please tell them to me."
> (Genesis chapter 40 verse 8)

Dreamers
of
God

Chapter One

✑

My Journey with Dreams

The earliest dream that I can remember was when I was about five years of age living in upstate New York. I had just recently given my heart to Jesus at a charismatic Catholic service on a Saturday night. It was in the winter of that same year around the Thanksgiving holiday time (for those non-familiar readers, that is in the third week of November). It was a cold night and I had asked my mom for an extra blanket, as fuel was at a premium and the family was trying everything to keep the budget. As soon as my mother placed the blanket over me, I was sleeping and knew I was in a dream.

I started to dream that I was running through a forest and that I had been given a very important message to deliver. I needed to get help to come to the community, as we were under attack. I was sent because I was small and could run fast. The thought in the dream, was that the leaders in the community believed I would go unnoticed by those wanting to get into the community. The village had high timber walls all the way around it.

I was fascinated with anything to do with soldiers or cowboys and especially Native Americans. This dream was so vivid I can even to this day tell you every colour detail from start to finish, four decades later. I can feel the mood of the dream. I can still describe my white cotton shirt with two strings that would lace and tie in the front. I can tell you I carried an old-fashioned musket with a ram rod and powder horn, and that my pursuers were full grown and would howl after me, and scream and shout to scare me. There were four of them that came after me and I just kept trying to get through the thickets, trees and branches. I won't go into all of the dream in this book, but at an early age God was speaking into my life.

This was actually a spiritual warfare dream, and God was trying to help me understand that there were forces who wanted to stop me from getting the message to others to help people. This has been true over and over again and for any person, no matter where they are from, the enemy of our soul hates us, and at times chases after us, to try to stop us from doing what we are called to do in Christ Jesus.

This is no less true for children, where the enemy shows his plot against their young lives. I woke up knowing exactly what the dream meant, and told my mother who listened and encouraged me to pray asking God for confirmation.

I would hear people describe their dreams to different people, and there would be several dreams I would know the keys to and be able to give the meaning.

This really started to happen for me at the age of six and seven. I had been baptised in the power of the Holy Spirit when I was six years old. There were certain gifts of the Holy Spirit that I would hear about and see going on in our Christian community, but no one mentioned dream interpretation.

There were no seminars or conferences, no books recommended, events or teachings on the subject when I was growing up. I was taught in picture format by the Lord. Then there was, what I call, "knowings," where God downloaded meaning to me on the spot of what the dream meant as a whole, or what the symbols, numbers and colours meant within the dream etc.

I was always fascinated with colours and details. I loved army men and soldiers and would love to look at the old paintings and drawings of soldier's uniforms from the old wars. I would know the different shades of colour. The crayons in the Crayola box set was like a huge gift, as I would try to use every colour and remember the different names of the colours. My dad was a highly successful, winning high school coach and I loved remembering each opponent's school name, colours and mascot. It was so interesting for me. Little did I know, God was training me through my likes, wants, desires and dreams to pay attention to detail.

As I grew older and started to read the Bible for myself, I would be interested in all the different objects, topics and elements used in Scripture. I remember reading the Bible, being in awe of everything that was mentioned in there, and the Holy Spirit gave me the following Scripture:

Thus, it is written, "The first man Adam became a

living being"; the last Adam became a life-giving spirit. But it is not the spiritual that is first but the natural, and then the spiritual. (1 Corinthians chapter 15 verses 45-46)

This was one of the greatest lessons I learned by the Holy Spirit talking to me as a young teenager, where He told me that there is spiritual meaning behind natural things. This has been a great blessing to my life and has brought amazing understanding as to how God speaks and communicates to the hearts of people. We know by reading that verse in the book of 1 Corinthians chapter 15, verse 46, that Adam was created by God, (Father, Son Jesus Christ, and The Holy Spirit). The second Adam is Jesus Christ, who redeemed what was tainted by sin because of the natural Adam's disobedience to God's command.

We can see in Scripture where there are a lot of types, shadows, foreshadowing, prophetic words and pictures that herald what is to come. Joshua is a type of Jesus Christ, Moses is another type of Jesus Christ the deliverer. When you look at the Tabernacle of Moses and see all the different colours, symbols and lengths of things, and see they all represent a hidden meaning, the natural thing speaks about a spiritual meaning.

The candlestick can be read about in Exodus chapter 25 verses 31-40. The candlestick definitely represents God's Word, being made out of gold and was the only light within the Holy place section of the tabernacle of Moses.

Make a lampstand of pure gold and hammer it out, base and shaft; its flower-like cups, buds and blossoms shall be of one piece with it. Six branches are to extend from the sides of the lampstand—three on one side and three on the other. Three cups shaped like almond flowers with buds and blossoms are to be on one branch, three on the next branch, and the same for all six branches extending from the lampstand. And on the lamp stand there are to be four cups shaped like almond flowers with buds and blossoms. One bud shall be under the first pair of branches extending from the lampstand, a second bud under the second pair, and a third bud under the third pair— six branches in all. The buds and branches shall all be of one piece with the lampstand, hammered out of pure gold. Then make its seven lamps and set them up on it so that they light the space in front of it. Its wick trimmers and trays are to be of pure gold. A talent of pure gold is to be used for the lampstand and all these accessories. See that you make them according to the pattern shown you on the mountain. (NIV)

God instructed Moses to make a lampstand that had seven branches—three branches on each side of a centre branch. On each of the branches were to be three cups (in the form of flowers) and each cup had buds and blossoms. The centre branch had four cups with each cup, again, having buds and blossoms.

The total number of decorations on each of the outer branches is therefore nine (three cups/flowers, three buds and three blossoms). The total number of decorations in the centre branch is 12 (four cups/flowers, four buds and four blossoms).

So, if you added them all up? $9 + 9 + 9 + 12 + 9 + 9 + 9 = 66$. The lamp stand is a picture of the Word of God and there are 66 books in

God's Word, the Bible, that gives light to all that would read and study its words!

It even gets more detailed, because, when we take a closer look, and were to take the first four branches, we get 39 (9 + 9 + 9 + 12). There are 39 books in the Old Testament. The remaining three branches give us 27 (9 + 9 + 9) which speaks of the 27 books in the New Testament. Pretty outstanding design by God alone. And remember that the lamp stand was made of pure gold. So, too, is the Word of God. The Bible is a divinely inspired book!

It has been extremely fun, and not boring in any way, to study metaphoric language, the symbols and meanings through dreams and visions and Scriptures, too numerous to mention. The entire Bible is a picture of God's love for you and me.

One instance that I will always remember in the area of dream interpretation, happened on an aeroplane from Sydney to the Sunshine Coast, Queensland. I was sitting next to a young woman and we started to talk. She asked me what I did and immediately out of my mouth came, "I'm a dream interpreter". I had just been in Sydney, Australia, at a weekend of meetings discussing and training in the area of dreams and visions, with a biblical perspective.

This woman was so interested, she began to tell me her heritage and her need to go to spiritualists and different mediums for direction. I told her I didn't need to do so because, I believed there was a living God who wanted to share his direction for our lives and, at times, He gave people dreams. She asked if she could tell me two dreams she recently had, that were almost bothering her. She could not stop thinking about them and felt they were significant.

On that plane I gave her suggestions of what the dreams meant, in my opinion, and she began to feel a peace and a relief. She believed that the answers I gave were true and it brought, not only tears to her eyes, but a relief to her heart. Friends, I can't explain everything about God. I know He is way bigger than my understanding and, even the attempt to understand. This woman who was in such need of true love and value, self-worth and identity, and everything that goes along with happiness and true joy, found an encounter with Jesus Christ right there and then, on the plane.

When we landed, she introduced me to her relative who was picking her up at the airport. I introduced her to my wife, and we invited her to come along to a meeting we were having at our home later in the week. She came with a family member and committed her life, fully and totally, to Jesus Christ right there sitting at our kitchen table. We still hear from her. She attends a great church in the Sydney area, was water baptised and encountered the power of the Holy Spirit in her life. She is leading her children in Christ and has influenced untold numbers, in a very successful role she has in the greater Sydney area, all from a dream being interpreted.

I'm not a salesman or one to say this always works like this, or, if you do it that way or this way then this will be the result. My point is that I want to encourage you to, please, follow the direction of the Holy Spirit in your life. The Holy Spirit is God, and I love Him and His ways so much.

Chapter Two

The Communicative God

God is a God of communication. God loves humanity so much He communicates to us, even when we don't perceive it or get what He is conveying to us. In the book of Job chapter 33 verses 13-15, this is spelled out clearly:

> Why do you contend with Him? For He does not give an accounting of any of His words. For God may speak in one way, or in another, Yet, man does not perceive it. In a dream, in a vision of the night, when deep sleep falls upon men, while men slumbering on their beds... (NKJV)

God can use anything to speak to humanity. He tends to be relentless, in my opinion. 1 John chapter 4 verses 7 and 8 says:

> Beloved, let us love one another, for love is of God;

and everyone who loves is born of God and knows God. He who does not love does not know God, for God is love.

God is motivated by who He is, which is love. God loves us so much he pursues us in offering relationship, desiring for us to acknowledge the offer and receive the invitation of relationship through his only Son Jesus Christ. God will use, music, conversation with others, Scripture, prayer, worship, events, movie clips, everyday situations, prophecy, our enemies, real life situations, coincidences, billboards, and anything else He wants to use to get our attention and deliver His message of love to us.

Not all of the communication God delivers is spoken or heard while awake, but sometimes the communication happens while a person is fast asleep.

Dreams tend to be symbolic and use metaphoric language. One needs to be curious in attitude and approach, to search out the meanings hidden within dreams. The dreamer can be given the interpretation immediately upon waking and some even have the meaning gained while in the dream.

Then there are the dreams where the interpretation needs to be asked from the giver of the dream. If the source is God, then only God can give the interpretation, but it is my belief, God can also tell the dreamer if it is a soul-initiated dream, or a dream from the enemy of our soul.

There are only three sources of all dreams; God, the Devil, or soul dreams, which are from the dreamer's condition within their soul. The Bible is full of instances of dreams and visions being a tool God uses to communicate to a person. There are many reasons for dreams. The reasons can be multi-applied to one dream; there can be dreams that seem to follow along—one to another in a night. There are even re-occurring dreams.

It should probably be mentioned, that dreams and visions are not the exact same thing, yet they both use metaphoric, or picture language to depict meaning. Visions tend to be more literal in meaning, where dreams are more symbolic. The book of Revelation is a prime example where the book has metaphoric imagery, but it is literal events that take place.

Interpretation of dreams by human effort and reasoning is an impossible thing to accomplish. In Genesis chapter 40 verse 8, Joseph states bare truth of the matter pertaining to dream interpretation—only God can give the interpretation to dreams.

> And they said to him, "We each have had a dream, and there is no interpreter of it". So, Joseph said to them, "Do not interpretations belong to God? Tell them to me, please". (NKJV)

It should be noted that not all dreams are from God. There are many dreams that, we would say, are from a chemical enhancement or the condition both positive or negative, weighing on a person's soul. The soul is made up of a person's mind, will and emotions. The soul is a powerful part of who we are as beings and can influence our dreams. Dark dreams, or those influenced by evil forces working against humanity, can also initiate dreams.

God wants to share His heart and intentions with people. We see well over 200 Scriptures that involve God engaging through a dream or a vision. The wonderful good news is, that God loves us and wants us to be encouraged in our life. I believe God can use any dream we may have. In the instance of any demonic influenced dream, He wants us to gain relationship and authority in Jesus Christ to be able to shut those types of dreams down! If we are having a negative dream, because we are anxious about a subject or worried, then God wants us to be aware; He wants us to be free from the worry or anxiety that can cause us to dream, accordingly.

A God dream is where God wants to make His thoughts and perhaps, His heart on a subject known to us, that possibly we miss when awake. There are numerous reasons for dreams, but dreams from God show us in the moment what is important to God. We are left to try to write down our dreams and then ask the Holy Spirit for understanding.

> In the first year of Belshazzar king of Babylon, Daniel had a dream and visions of his head while on his bed. Then he wrote down the dream, telling the main facts. (Daniel chapter 7 verse 1 NKJV)

It is impossible for man to take symbolic language and then try to put it into an understandable format and language. It can only be accomplished by the understanding given from the Holy Spirit. Why not ask God to give you understanding of a dream that might be puzzling you?

Chapter Three

Abraham's Vision

Genesis chapter 15

Everyone can remember where they were when traumatic, globally shocking events have taken place. People can tell me where they were and what they were doing when John F. Kennedy was assassinated in Dallas, Texas. If I were to say to you the numeric phrase 9/11, you would instantly be able to tell me where you were, how old you were, what happened, and how you came to know when the towers were attacked in New York City on September 11th, 2001. I remember when David Wilkerson, from Time Square Church, had a vision where he saw New York City burning and under attack. This was, without a doubt, a God-warning and for the expressed purpose of getting people to pray for the city and its inhabitants.

I had a vision late in the year of 1999, of the twin towers being hit in New York City. I actually had told a few people that I couldn't get rid of the imagery—it was disturbing, and really didn't make sense to me. So, I began to pray for the city. I had never had quite an experience like it. I went to trusted people with it and they encouraged me to pray to see if God spoke anything more to me. So, by faith I prayed. Then on September 11, 2001, almost 24 months later, it actually happened.

My point being, that God does give visions, and I thought it best to discuss a vision before we actually dig deeper into dreams. Why would we discuss a vision when the title of this book is "Dreamers of God?" Well, most things that pertain to God in the area of communication, and subjects about spiritual topics, have a convergence. It is very difficult to put things into nice, neat, clean separated boxes. We love our, "God boxes," but God doesn't really fit into those boxes!

When we talk about dreams, it's going to also include visions. God speaks definitely through the Bible. The Holy Spirit, who is God, speaks to men's hearts and will even give impressions, which are pictures or inward visions, to a person. Then there is the use of angelic encounters which are mentioned throughout the Bible. So, it is very hard to just focus on one subject like dreams, and not cross into other spiritual things.

Abram who later was renamed Abraham, had a vision from God where he was reminded that he would have a son and be the father of many nations.

> No longer shall your name be called Abram, but your name shall be Abraham; for I have made you a father of many nations. (Genesis chapter 17 verse 5 NKJV)

Let's have a look in the book of Genesis, at chapter 15

verse 1. Abram has a vision where he is told to fear not!

> After these things the word of the Lord came to
> Abram in a vision, saying, "Do not be afraid, Abram.
> I am your shield, your exceedingly great reward".
> (NKJV)

When we encounter God, it can be fearful, and not just warm fuzzy feelings. When Job has an encounter with God in the book of Job chapter 4 verses 12-15, the hair stands on end on his body because the glory of God, unveiled, is a daunting, filled-with-awe, moment.

> Now a word was secretly brought to me, and my ear
> received a whisper of it. In disquieting thoughts from
> the visions of the night, when deep sleep falls on men,
> fear came upon me, and trembling, which made all
> my bones shake. Then a spirit passed before my face;
> The hair on my body stood up. (NKJV)

God tells Abram that He is Abram's shield and exceeding great reward. A shield represents protection. Abram had won battles and seen giants defeated, in Genesis chapter 14 verses 5-11:

> In the fourteenth year Chedorlaomer and the kings
> that were with him came and attacked the Rephaim
> in Ashteroth Karnaim, the Zuzim in Ham, the Emim
> in Shaveh Kiriathaim, and the Horites in their
> mountain of Seir, as far as El Paran, which is by the
> wilderness. Then they turned back and came to En
> Mishpat (that is, Kadesh), and attacked all the country
> of the Amalekites, and also the Amorites who dwelt in
> Hazezon Tamar.

17

And the king of Sodom, the king of Gomorrah, the king of Admah, the king of Zeboiim, and the king of Bela (that is, Zoar) went out and joined together in battle in the Valley of Siddim against Chedorlaomer king of Elam, Tidal king of nations, Amraphel king of Shinar, and Arioch king of Ellasar—four kings against five. Now the Valley of Siddim was full of asphalt pits; and the kings of Sodom and Gomorrah fled; some fell there, and the remainder fled to the mountains. Then they took all the goods of Sodom and Gomorrah, and all their provisions, and went their way. (NKJV)

God had declared the prophetic word over Abram's life, in Genesis chapter 13 verses 15-1:

"...for all the land which you see I give to you and your descendants forever. And I will make your descendants as the dust of the earth; so that if a man could number the dust of the earth then your descendants also could be numbered. Arise, walk in the land through its length and its width, for I give it to you." Then Abram moved his tent and went and dwelt by the terebinth trees of Mamre, which are in Hebron, and built an altar there to the Lord. (NKJV)

God says that He would make his seed "as the dust of the earth", meaning that no one would be able to count the number of his offspring. Therefore, by looking at imagery language or picture language, as I like to describe it, we can say that when we see dust in a dream, it could hold the meaning of uncountable or unmeasurable. We are basing this possible meaning upon what we see in Scripture.

God loves humanity so much He speaks in

multiple ways to us. Why would He do this? So we can
have multiple opportunities to capture what He is trying
to convey to us. When we look in Job, chapter 33 verses
14-16, what does this really mean?

> For God may speak in one way, or in another, yet
> man does not perceive it. In a dream, in a vision of
> the night, when deep sleep falls upon men, while
> slumbering on their beds, then He opens the ears of
> men, and seals their instruction. (NKJV)

It means that God wants us to receive what He is
communicating to us! God loves us so much that He
will repeat Himself and use different avenues or ways,
to let us know what He is communicating. God will even
remind us of what He has said, so we don't lose hope
(expectation), or become distracted in life. Therefore,
God will use a dream or a vision, to direct us or warn us
in a situation. I believe He uses the time when we are a
captive audience, while we are sleeping.

In verse 16 of chapter 33 in Job, it says that God
opens up our ears so that we can hear what God is saying
to our lives. We need our spiritual ears open to His voice.
John chapter 10 verse 10 (paraphrased); 'His sheep know
and recognise the voice of the Shepherd!'

The recognition of a voice takes time. God wants
to take the time with us so that we learn to recognise His
voice in our lives. HE wants us taking the time, to train
our soul and spirit to recognise His word, by reading
Scripture through relationship in Jesus Christ! He wants
us to spend time with Him in our prayer time, developing
a listening skill, as well as an ability to share our heart
and thoughts with God. The point being, spending time

with God is what builds our relationship with Him! There are no substitutes for hanging out with God in our daily life routines!

God, because he loves Abram, and the important plan that God has chosen to use Abram in, prophesies to Abram in Genesis 13 and then He gives him a literal vision to remind him of God's plan for his life. I really love that Abram was interacting with God within the vision that was unfolding for him. Abram asks God in the middle of a vision 'what will you give me?' Abram knew God as his protection, but hadn't seen the fulfilment in his opinion of the great reward, which referred to his seed being like dust. He hadn't seen the fulfilment of the picture language he knew was from God Himself.

Abram says, 'I have gone childless and you have given me no seed and I have no heir to the riches I have'. In the book of Genesis chapter 13 verse 2, "Abram was very rich in livestock, in silver, and in gold".

It states clearly, he was very wealthy in cattle, silver and gold. Isn't that just like us? We get impatient! No matter the resource God uses to convey the message, when we receive a promise or a prophecy from God, we usually think it is immediately right then and there that it will happen. Patience is usually not our virtue, but learned, and applied by God using time.

God then speaks to Abram, in the book of Genesis chapter 15 verse 4, 'And behold, the word of the Lord came to him, saying, "This one shall not be your heir, but one who will come from your own body shall be your heir." (NKJV)

The word of the Lord came unto him, telling Abram that the heir that was not from his own blood was not the heir, but one who was coming from within him. What? The one yet to come was to be the heir! If I were Abram, I might be a little confused. God knows us so well, being our designer, He shows Abram more, so he can understand.

So, then He takes Abram and tells him to look upward into the sky or up to heaven. You know that's the best perspective! God will take us and change our view. The heavens can sometimes represent revelation, which can only come from God. It is a positional change God is trying to get Abram to understand.

God wants Abram to believe in the Word of God for his life! God wants us to do the same. I believe God has a prophecy over each life and in our free will that God has distributed to each person on earth, we need to make a choice to trust and believe what God has said about us.

God shows Abram the stars and tells Abram that his offspring, his children, will be like the number of the stars that he can see. Abram of course cannot number them, and we call this 'the multitudes'. In the book of Genesis chapter 15 verse 6, Abram believed in the Lord; and he counted it to him for righteousness. God is after our belief in Him. The vision that Abram has comes to pass, as all those who believe in the Lordship and Saviour, Jesus Christ, becomes a son or daughter of Abraham, through their belief. Therefore, the vision is literal, and it is still being continually added to and fulfilled by those who freely ask Jesus to forgive their sins and call upon the name of the Lord and Saviour, Jesus!

We can place this dream in the category of a *calling dream* or a *directional dream*. Because of the love He has for this man, God reminds Abram using another imagery; instead of dust God shows him stars. Interestingly, God can use two different objects or pictures to show the same meaning. Because of Abram's belief in what God said to him, it is counted as righteousness to Abram. It is important for us as followers of Christ to believe in the confirmed direction of God. Later, unfortunately, Abram is distracted by Sarai who tries by human effort to make the word of God happen practically, which ends up in a terrible mess starting in Genesis chapter 16, but that is a different story.

Abram continues though, to have a wonderful encounter with God where God causes a deep sleep to come upon Abram.

> Now when the sun was going down, a deep sleep fell upon Abram; and behold, horror and great darkness fell upon him. (Genesis chapter 15 verse 12 NASB)

Abram, actually, will see the captivity of the Israelites in Egypt as slaves for a 400-year duration. The amazing fact that the captivity will not begin for another 400 years is also a wonderful event.

So, a great and powerful God has a relationship in the Old Testament with Abram, to the point where there is dialogue back and forth from God to Abram. In this ongoing interaction through relationship, Abram is shown an event that won't begin for 400 years and will last for 400 years, where Israel would be slaves to the Egyptians but would come out of the land with great substance of resources. This part of the event where they leave with riches, happens 800 years in the future from the point of the dream...well after Abram is named

Abraham and dies in peace and of an old age.

> Now as for you, you shall go to your fathers in
> peace; you shall be buried at a good old age. (Genesis
> chapter 15 verse 15 NKJV)

Why would God do such a thing? Why does God show a
man an event yet to be started for 400 years, that would
last for 400 years? What is the point? God uses a vision
as the medium or way, to release prophetic insight about
the future, that only God could have known.

God wants witnesses to the truth that He alone
is God. God wants to show what is going to happen
before it happens in relationship with people. It clearly
shows God knows exactly what will happen and when
it will take place. God is omnipresent and sits above
the dimension of time. God is sharing this revelation to
prove that Abram's seed which is under captivity would
also see freedom and blessing, and it is part of the answer
to the question that Abram has earlier. Abram wants to
know about his great reward and God shows him the
answer to his question using a deep sleep and a dream.

In dreams and visions God can answer our
heartfelt questions about things we have yet to see
fulfilled answers to. God uses visions and dreams to
get the direct point into our understanding and for it
to become revelation, so that we believe the plan and
destiny God has for our life.

Chapter Four

⁓

Abimelech

Genesis chapter 20

verses 1–7

In Genesis chapter 20 verses 1-7, there is a weird story of the time when Abraham, who used to be called Abram, had a wife Sarah who was incredibly beautiful. Abraham and Sarah travel south, which is actually the second time he does. You can read about his first journey in Genesis chapter 13. Abraham and Sarah go to a place called Gerar. There a king rules who is not a follower of Yahweh. He has multiple wives and wants to take Sarah as one of his wives.

Abraham calls Sarah his sister and not his wife, allowing the king to believe she was available to be added as his wife. And Abraham journeyed from there to the South, and dwelt between Kadesh and Shur, and stayed in Gerar. Now Abraham said of Sarah his wife, "She is my sister." And Abimelech king of Gerar sent and took Sarah. But God came to Abimelech in a dream by night, and said to him, "Indeed you are a dead man because of the woman whom you have taken, for she is a man's wife." But Abimelech had not come near her; and he said, "Lord, will You slay a righteous nation also? Did he not say to me, 'She is my sister'? And she, even she herself said, 'He is my brother'. In the integrity of my heart and innocence of my hands I have done this." And God said to him in a dream, "Yes, I know that you did this in the integrity of your heart. For I also withheld you from sinning against Me; therefore, I did not let you touch her. Now therefore, restore the man's wife; for he is a prophet, and he will pray for you and you shall live. But if you do not restore her, know that you shall surely die, you and all who are yours. (Genesis chapter 20 verse 2 NASB)

This is a classic case of a warning dream. God intervenes in the life of the king and gives the king a dream. Looking at Genesis chapter 20 verse 3 and verse 6, the Hebrew word used for the word dream is *'Khal-ome'*— the meaning for this particular word is connected to the idea that there is a prophetic meaning attached to the dream, and it is why this word is used specifically. This word is used 65 times in the Scriptures. In this chapter it is used twice, and God gives prophetic revelation as a warning to a non-believing king! Here we see the amazing heart of God to preserve life and bless people, even those who are not yet following Him in a godly devoted lifestyle. Later, amazingly Isaac does the same thing his father did and introduces his wife Rebekah as his sister. Rebekah who was extraordinarily beautiful, was with Isaac during a time of famine. Isaac called Rebekah his sister in

Genesis chapter 26, allowing history to repeat itself in the next generation.

Now, back to Abraham, I believe he was motivated by fear. I believe that Abraham was afraid that the ruler would kill him and take his wife for himself. In this dispensation of time, the rules of relationships and marriages were very different than during the Israelite captivity and beyond. In truth, Sarah was Abraham's half-sister (see Genesis chapter 20 verse 12). Yet, God allowed this to take place in that day. Once again, this book isn't about these details, sorry!

Looking now again, at Genesis chapter 20 verses 4-5:

> But Abimelech had not come near her; and he said, "Lord, will You slay a righteous nation also? Did he not say to me, 'She is my sister'? And she, even she herself said, 'He is my brother'. In the integrity of my heart and innocence of my hands I have done this. (NKJV)

God comes in a dream to the ruler of the land, Abimelech, and warns him that the woman he has taken is, in fact, Abraham's wife. God states to the king he is a dead man, because the woman that he has taken into the concubine chambers is another man's wife and not his sister. Once again, I believe it is fascinating that Abimelech has a conversation with God in the dream!

In the book of Genesis chapter 20 verse 4, the dialogue between the heathen King Abimelech and Almighty God, was of Abimelech explaining that, both Abraham and Sarah said she was Abraham's sister. Abimelech is saying to God, 'so this is not my fault and

I haven't done anything wrong!' Imagine, that he even pleads his case of innocence to Almighty God in a dream being a polygamist and polytheist.

In Genesis chapter 20, verse 6, God clearly shares with the dreamer, Abimelech, by using the dream as the form of communication. God says to Abimelech, *I know that you did this thing innocently*. God intervenes and shows two things about Himself, the first is that He is kind, and the second that God sees all, by not letting Abimelech touch Sarah. God stops Abimelech from pursuing Sarah. God is revealing that He is merciful, and does so by the dream given, to a worshipper of false gods.

Sarah is going to be the mother of the promise of God to Abraham. God uses a warning dream, that brings revelation to the ruler of what is really going on in this whole situation. I love how God preserves the womb of the woman so as not to be defiled. I love how God protects the plan that allows Abraham and Sarah to be partners with God.

In verse 7 God tells the king that Abraham is a prophet and that he needs to return the woman to her husband, that the prophet will pray for him, and that Abimelech will live. Remember, Abimelech was dead, a dead man to God. God restates that if Abimelech does not return her untouched, he will die and everyone around him. Early the next morning, the ruler told all his servants what had happened and they were all afraid with the fear of the Lord.

A warning dream is for the purpose of making a change in direction and action. Here we have Abimelech, a heathen king following and worshipping other gods, but he gets the point loud and clear from God, and he immediately makes things right. This is the purpose of a warning dream should you ever receive one.

Abimelech calls for Abraham and asks him why he did this thing? Abraham replies, saying, he knew that the fear of the Lord was not in the place where they were; he was afraid for his life and that Sarah would be taken from him. Abimelech makes a prophetic action using sacrifices and restores Sarah back to her husband.

Now God answers Abraham's prayer, on behalf of Abimelech. Abimelech and his wife were healed, and all the maidservants received the blessing to be able to have children. God had closed up the wombs of the house of Abimelech because of what had happened with Sarah, see Genesis chapter 20 verse 17:

> Then Abraham prayed to God, and God healed Abimelech, and also healed his wife and female slaves so that they bore children.

God is so much greater than our latent fears and the vows we make in life. Abraham had a plan to take matters into his own hands as he and his wife travelled. Abraham had a premeditated plan of action which was to call Sarah his sister.

> And when God caused me to wander from my father's house, I said to her, "This is the kindness you must do me: at every place to which we come, say of me, "He is my brother." (Genesis chapter 20 verse 13)

Man has his plans that can negate or ruin the plan of the Lord, because God has given humanity a free will and, there are no guarantees the plan of God automatically is completed.

What if Sarah had been taken by the ruler and became pregnant or defiled? We see in chapter 21 of Genesis, that Sarah becomes pregnant by Abraham, straight after this account with Abimelech. There are many times when we are confronted with decisions in various situations when an alternative choice is presented to us, directly before the Lord's timing for the miraculous or breakthrough. In God's mercy and grace, He extended a warning to a ruler and the heathen ruler ends up being blessed for listening to the warning! Thankfully, Sarah becomes the mother of God's chosen people and the rest, as they say, is His story!

Chapter Five

Jacob

Genesis chapter 28
verses 10–17

Jacob, which means 'supplanter', enacts the meaning of his name, in that he was a deceiver. He is seen as being helped by his mother to steal his brother's birthright, Esau's inheritance. Esau's anger is huge, to the degree that Jacob flees from his brother. Jacob, who escapes his brother's fury, finds himself on a necessary journey but going to an unknown location. Jacob comes to a sacred place of consecration, unaware that it is the exact place where Abraham, in a time past, placed stones to mark the place where he had encountered a living God.

In this place, with a sacred stone for his pillows, Jacob has a dream initiated by God. As I previously mentioned, there are many different reasons for dreams. God, in this encounter with Jacob through the use of a dream, is affirming His covenant with Abraham, that continues through Jacob's destiny and life on earth.

Genesis chapter 28 verse 12 says: *"And he dreamed"*...
the word 'dreamed' here, is the Hebrew word *'khaw-lam'*, which means to make robust or strong. This dream then, by definition of the original wording, has been used for the purpose of making Jacob stronger. This would be categorised as a strengthening dream. God strengthens us in Himself. It is not the dream that does the strengthening, but the Father God using a dream to bring strength to the dreamer. It's God Himself we stand in awe of, not the different things or ways He uses to reveal Himself.

The imagery Jacob sees in the dream is a ladder set up on the earth, with the top of it reaching to heaven; and he sees the angels of God ascending and descending on the ladder. The Hebrew word used for 'ladder', is *cullam.* The meaning is, to pile up like the picture of terraces or, in other words, a stairway to heaven. Let's take a look in the book of John at chapter 1, verse 51:

> And he said to him, "Truly, truly, I say to you, you will see heaven opened, and the angels of God ascending and descending on the Son of Man."

This is the account of Jesus ministering to Nathanael. Jesus gives him a prophesy that we never see written about or discussed afterward. Jesus tells Nathanael that he would see heaven open and the angels of God ascending and descending upon the Son of man.

Once again looking at the dream Jacob had, we can find ourselves in an unfolding plan of God upon or within a family, generationally. The eternal plan of God for the family of Abraham extends beyond the actual days that Abraham lived on earth. It would extend to Abraham's son Isaac, and later his grandson Jacob. Jacob doesn't have a clue, it seems, as to the geographical place he finds himself in while laying on the actual earth. He has no idea that this location and the stone 'pillow' is the place of remembrance to the covenant made with his grandfather, Abraham, years ago. Jacob is reminded by the Lord Himself what his destiny is in life, which is to see "his own seed number like the dust", (Genesis chapter 28 verse 14). The same metaphoric language is used with the word 'dust'. The same symbolism used that his grandfather Abraham received from God, 'dust' to depict innumerable offspring.

Sometimes the dreams we have been given allow us to get a glimpse into our destiny on earth. Here Jacob is given a front seat to see what God's intention is for his life in some part. Jacob is given an affirmation by God in the dream. God can use dreams to tell the dreamer that He supports, protects, directs and/or affirms the dreamer.

My desire is not to make dreams 'the be all and end all' of things God uses in our life to get our attention. My intention is that we start to become intentional about our thanksgiving for God, and fall deeper in love with Him and His marvellous ways!

Jacob was given a dream to allow him to understand that he was an important part of the plan of God to use him and his family line, to fulfil the plan of God on earth. Jacob would later get a name change, in Genesis chapter 32. Jacob became Israel because he wrestled with God and won. God changed his nature, character, name and heart. May we allow God to do the same in us all!

Chapter Six

⁓

Laban

Genesis chapter 31
verse 24

Here is a small portion of Scripture that could easily get overlooked by a reader of Scripture. Laban is Jacob's father-in-law and has tricked Jacob with his daughter's, Leah and Rachel. There has been family turmoil and a plot that has been unfolded by Laban. This has caused great tension in the family dynamics; with resentment and betrayal, love and support, all having been ingredients in the mix of these relationships.

God gives Laban an instructional dream at night, where God tells Laban to be careful not to say anything to Jacob, either good or bad. Take a look in the book of Genesis chapter 31, verses 22-30:

> And Laban was told on the third day that Jacob had fled. Then he took his brethren with him and pursued

him for seven days' journey, and he overtook him in the mountains of Gilead. But God had come to Laban the Syrian in a dream by night, and said to him, "Be careful that you speak to Jacob neither good nor bad."

So, Laban overtook Jacob. Now Jacob had pitched his tent in the mountains, and Laban with his brethren pitched in the mountains of Gilead.
And Laban said to Jacob: "What have you done, that you have stolen away unknown to me, and carried away my daughters like captives taken with the sword? Why did you flee away secretly, and steal away from me, and not tell me; for I might have sent you away with joy and songs, with timbrel and harp? And you did not allow me to kiss my sons and my daughters. Now you have done foolishly in so doing. It is in my power to do you harm, but the God of your father spoke to me last night, saying, "Be careful that you speak to Jacob neither good nor bad." And now you have surely gone because you greatly long for your father's house, but why did you steal my gods?' (NKJV)

Looking now at verse 24:

But God had come to Laban the Syrian in a dream by night, and said to him, "Be careful that you speak to Jacob neither good nor bad."

I want to bring attention to the phrase 'a dream by night'. Does this infer that one can have a dream in the night as a comparison to a dream during the day?

I just pose the question to be able to reflect on this point I make, to stimulate the ability to ask God questions. A good question can be a wonderful asset in the hands of the curious believer. The hungry heart of a believer allows there to be a position of seeking or searching deeper, than leaving this at just surface level. I find it helpful for me to write down and ask the Holy Spirit for answers to questions, that are stimulated as I read through Scripture.

God gives Laban, the dreamer, specific instructions in the dream not to speak to Jacob, good or bad. God tells Laban to be careful—in other words, to pay attention and be intentional in how he speaks to Jacob and treats him. If you read further in this chapter, Jacob really speaks his mind to Laban of how he has been treated, and why he would run away from Laban at the chance given to him and Rachael.

Sometimes dreams can be for the expressed purpose of God telling us how He wants us to act, or how God wants the dreamer to respond, in certain situations. It has become apparent in my own life that, during a dream, God decides to share things with me and I'm a captive audience for Him to express His view on a subject. I could be intentionally, or unintentionally, dismissing or deflecting the communication he has been trying to convey to me, because of my stubbornness or contrary opinion on a topic.

God knows exactly what is coming during this unfolding scenario, with regard to the life of these people. God knows that Jacob is going to just let loose, with a barrage of words and expressed feelings, toward his father-in-law. God sees all, is before all, is all powerful! He instructs Laban, so that he would react according to the will of God and not in his own soulish will.

Laban even recounts to Jacob what happened to him in the dream, see verse 29:

> It is in my power to do you harm, but the God of your father spoke to me last night, saying, "Be careful that you speak to Jacob neither good nor bad."

Laban has taken note, very clearly, of what was required by him from God concerning this whole situation. This is encouraging to us as we read this portion of Scripture. It shows that man does have the ability to be instructed by God in a dream. Laban, to his credit, in the direct moment not only received the instruction but remembered the instructions and could recount them.

God has an uncanny way of instructing people in ways that are not only fascinating, but very practical. Laban had treated Jacob unjustly, in so many ways, previous to this chapter. God is looking for an end to this scenario that is just and right, according to God's plan for these people. God intervenes when it is absolutely necessary, so that this heated relationship will not explode to the next level, and only God knows what could have been the results.

Chapter Seven

Joseph

Genesis chapter 37
verses 1–11

There are two men in Scripture that clearly possessed the gift or ability to interpret dreams. The first is Joseph, found in Genesis chapter 37. He is one of those 'weird' people that the church of modern day sometimes shuns or misunderstands. We see in this chapter where he is 17 years old, just a teenager, and has the favour of his father, Jacob. This caused a huge division between Joseph and his brothers. It was a dream Joseph had, that was the cause of such a severe reaction of jealousy. His brothers plotted to pretend he was killed and sold him into slavery, then to be taken to a far-off nation.

Joseph was given a dream where he sees, through symbolic language used in the dream, his family bowing to him in respect. Joseph naively shares this with his family. Joseph innocently shares the dream once again, and this time his brothers are moved to terrible acts, due to their uncontrolled jealousy toward Joseph. Can the dreams of God cause there to be jealousy against the dreamer? It has been my experience, that yes, this can still happen.

Joseph might have gloated to his brothers, maybe he communicated to his brothers in a prideful manner? Whatever happened, the true feelings that his brothers did possess about him came out. There are a number of people whom I have encountered, that use this specific passage and have speculated about the mood conveyed by the dreamer. Joseph might have been critical or prideful, but only God truly knows. However, speculation or not, we can use this moment to remind ourselves, we cannot be boastful in our delivery of what we feel God is telling us. It is the wonderful favour of God to us when He reveals things.

When Joseph shares his dream, it says that his brothers hated him even more.

> Now Joseph had a dream, and when he told it to his brothers they hated him even more. (Genesis chapter 37 verse 5)

Sometimes we get the idea that everyone will rejoice with our revelation and will celebrate us as we use our God given gifts and talents. The ability to interpret dreams is a God given ability. So, as Joseph is young and learning that God speaks to him in dreams, he has run straight into the jealousy of those who are competing with him, and he doesn't fully realise it.

Here in this portion of Scripture, we see two dreams are given to the dreamer and the imagery is completely different, but the meaning is still very much the same. In regard to Joseph's first dream, he sees sheaves bound together in a field, then a sheaf of wheat and sheaves of wheat, representing the brothers who bowed to Joseph's sheaf of wheat. This angered the brothers and brought out even more of a reaction of hatred toward their younger brother.

> He said to them, "Hear this dream that I have dreamed: Behold, we were binding sheaves in the field, and behold, my sheaf arose and stood upright. And behold, your sheaves gathered around it and bowed down to my sheaf." (Genesis chapter 37 verses 6 and 7)

The second dream Joseph has is illustrated by the sun and moon and 11 stars bowing down to Joseph. The sun represents his father, the moon his mother, and the stars once again represent his 11 brothers. When his father heard this dream, he rebuked Joseph but as it states in verse 11 of Genesis chapter 37, he kept these things in mind as he knew there might be something to the dream. His brothers, however, were tipped over the edge of jealousy into treachery.

> Then he dreamed another dream and told it to his brothers and said, "Behold, I have dreamed another dream. Behold, the sun, the moon, and eleven stars were bowing down to me." But when he told it to his father and to his brothers, his father rebuked him and said to him, "What is this dream that you have dreamed? Shall I and your mother and your brothers indeed come to bow ourselves to the ground before you?" And his brothers were jealous of him, but his

father kept the saying in mind. (Genesis chapter 37
verses 9-11)

There have been several occasions where I have been
able to reassure people who share their dreams with me,
that it is alright to have more than one dream in a night.
It is found in the Bible, in fact. There have been those
who have dreams that have no noticeable connection one
with another; those dreams that are like running stories,
it seems. Then there are others, like Joseph's dream,
where the meaning is the same using different imagery.

Joseph is plotted against by his brothers, sold
into slavery and taken eventually to Egypt. This would
have been an extremely scary time for young Joseph.
He found favour with God and men, eventually being
placed within Potiphar's house, then afterward, only to
be betrayed by the lies of Potiphar's wife and placed in
prison unjustly.

There is an example here in the life and times of
Joseph, that allows me to discuss how the giftings and
abilities that God gives us, does not diminish through
tough and stressful times. Prison would have been less
than glamourous in ancient Egypt. Here in Genesis
chapter 40, in the middle of being imprisoned for doing
the honourable thing and running away from Potiphar's
wife's sexual advances, Joseph meets the Pharaoh's
cupbearer and baker, who had been put into prison by
the leader of the nation.

I just want to pause here and remind us all, that
there is no position without a cost. God has paid the price
through His one and only Son Jesus Christ! However, God
uses brokenness as a tool to bring humility and reliance
upon Jesus. The element of suffering is something we do

not understand well and, in some circles, is altogether forgotten, misunderstood, or preached against. What we do know is, suffering produces perseverance, perseverance character, and character hope.

> Not only that, but we rejoice in our sufferings, knowing that suffering produces endurance, and endurance produces character, and character produces hope (Romans chapter 5, verses 3 and 4)

Genesis chapter 40 verses 5-8 tells us that, both the cupbearer and the baker have dreams on the same night in the prison. They wake up in the morning and are both deeply disturbed, because they have had these dreams and they don't know what they mean. Interestingly, they must have been in a culture that placed credence and importance in dreams. Dreams from God carry a sense of meaning with them. Some people say they carry a weight, and they can be irritating enough for us to try to find the meaning of them. A holy irritation, so to speak, can accompany a dream that is from God.

> And one night they both dreamed—the cupbearer and the baker of the king of Egypt, who were confined in the prison—each his own dream, and each dream with its own interpretation. When Joseph came to them in the morning, he saw that they were troubled. So, he asked Pharaoh's officers who were with him in custody in his master's house, "Why are your faces downcast today?" They said to him, "We have had dreams, and there is no one to interpret them." And Joseph said to them, "Do not interpretations belong to God? Please tell them to me." (Genesis chapter 40 verses 5-8)

Joseph tells them both to tell him the dreams, and mentions the truth that only God can give the interpretation of dreams, (Genesis chapter 40 verse 8). No matter how many dream books we study, or metaphoric language dictionaries we look at, we won't be able to get the true interpretation of what God intends, if we don't have the Holy Spirit giving us the answers. Our reliance is not in our training but in God, the Holy Spirit himself, to be able to tell us the meaning by faith, and not human effort or reasoning.

God wants to give a person understanding. It is my opinion, that God does not want to keep people in the dark all the time, even though God chooses to use mystery and hides secrets of the kingdom. Proverbs chapter 25, verse 2 says:

> It is the glory of God to conceal things, but the glory of kings is to search things out.

The Bible spells out for the reader, in the book of Revelation chapter 1 verse 6, that it is the intent of God, according to His plan, that the believer is actually considered a priest and a king unto his glory.

> And from Jesus Christ the faithful witness, the firstborn of the dead, and the ruler of kings on earth. To him who loves us and has freed us from our sins by his blood and made us a kingdom, priests to his God and Father, to him be glory and dominion forever and ever. Amen.

The book of Mark, chapter 4 verses 22-25, gives scriptural inference to the truth that God, even though He uses parabolic language and hides meaning in imagery and metaphoric language, really enjoys revealing more than concealing, and it is a way He gains glory.

> For nothing is hidden except to be made manifest; nor is anything secret except to come to light. If anyone has ears to hear, let him hear." And he said to them, "Pay attention to what you hear: with the measure you use, it will be measured to you, and still more will be added to you. For to the one who has, more will be given, and from the one who has not, even what he has will be taken away.

This portion of Scripture says, the more we use our abilities, for example spiritual hearing, the more accurate and acute it becomes. I love how our God is a God of abundance and he wants to add to what he has already given to each individual. It says in this passage as well, to pay attention to what you hear. In other words, make note of it, be intentional within our hearts to want to listen and pay attention, within our busy lives.

Chapter Eight

✦

The Chief Butler

Genesis chapter 40
verses 9–15

God has chosen how we are to live our life on earth. A component for living on earth is, that God continuously devises ways to communicate to a person. Psalm chapter 127, verse 2 says:

> It is in vain that you rise up early and go late to rest, eating the bread of anxious toil; for he gives to his beloved sleep.

It is God's intent that humanity rests and sleeps, and has a mode of communication that God can speak to our hearts, minds and spirits when we are sleeping.

God has chosen to use what seems to be a mystical way of speaking, and it is mysterious and hidden, with regard to dream language. However, God doesn't want to stay obscure. The heart of God is to be found by every individual, that has ever lived on the face of the earth. When we look in 2 Samuel chapter 14 verse 14, we get a picture of this amazing God who wants relationship with humanity.

> We must all die; we are like water spilled on the ground, which cannot be gathered up again. But God will not take away life, and he devises means so that the banished one will not remain an outcast.

Here we find deep in the Old Testament, the deliberate picture painted by God, Himself, that He does not want people estranged from him. It is His continual desire for people to be brought close to Him and be in relationship with him, through the atoning sacrifice of Jesus Christ, only by accepting what was paid for on the cross by Christ. God does give dreams to those who have yet to know him in relationship.

The cupbearer or Butler, as he is described in some versions of the Bible, tells his dream first to Joseph in the book of Genesis, chapter 40 verses 5 through 19. Remember, Joseph not only had dreams, but he could interpret dreams from God. Some people can interpret dreams of others. Truthfully, there will be people in the church who won't be able to interpret another's dream. Some people will have dreams from God and be able to get the interpretation from God for themselves; but they or others, will need the help of a person with the gifting to interpret dreams.

Looking at the dream of the Chief Butler in Scripture:

> In my dream there was a vine before me, and on the

vine, there were three branches. As soon as it budded, its blossoms shot forth, and the clusters ripened into grapes. Pharaoh's cup was in my hand, and I took the grapes and pressed them into Pharaoh's cup and placed the cup in Pharaoh's hand."

Then Joseph said to him, "This is its interpretation: the three branches are three days. In three days, Pharaoh will lift up your head and restore you to your office, and you shall place Pharaoh's cup in his hand as formerly, when you were his cupbearer. Only remember me, when it is well with you, and please do me the kindness to mention me to Pharaoh, and so get me out of this house. For I was indeed stolen out of the land of the Hebrews, and here also I have done nothing that they should put me into the pit. (Genesis chapter 40, verses 9-15)

I will mention this probably more than once, but God speaks in colloquial words and expressions. That means, that God speaks to us in ways we understand based on our education, our occupation, culture etc. You will notice later in this book that Gideon, who deals with grain, is given spiritual connotation and implication prophetically, by his encounter with the Angel using elements in everyday life that he can relate to. God gives us the spirit of understanding, not just revelation. In the book of Ephesians, chapter 1, verse 17, the whole reason for an encounter with God is to know Jesus better. Jesus is the door of salvation, and is the recognizable door to the eye that has been opened by faith.

So, to help humanity, God speaks in ways by which we can gain understanding or insight. God will even use slang to help us better understand the meaning. The meaning behind this dream from the cupbearer and the Chief Baker would be placed in the complex section of dream interpretation.

In regard to the dream that was given to the cupbearer who would be dealing with wine, a dream is given where wine and grapes are the objects, in order for the cupbearer to have the opportunity to relate to the meaning.

Joseph, only by the Holy Spirit giving him understanding, says that the three branches represents three days. How does Joseph know that the three branches are three days? Why not three months, three people, three years, three minutes? God gives Joseph an ear to hear accurately and tells the cupbearer that he will be let out of prison by Pharaoh in three days! What a bold statement to make!

How do we know the interpretation we gain is from the Lord? Well, first, I want to say that there is not a formula we can use. People often want a formula, especially, it seems to me, in Christianity. That way, we can know we are doing right and, perhaps, point to someone else who is doing it wrong or badly to justify ourselves? Hebrews chapter 11 verse 6 says:

> But without faith it is impossible to please Him, for
> he who comes to God must believe that He is, and that
> He is a rewarder of those who diligently seek Him.

To find what God hides takes searching! We need to be those who have, 'grit' or, to use another word, tenacity, to find the meaning from God!

This dream was a restoration dream for the life of the cupbearer. Joseph, desperate to get out of prison, uses the opportunity to remind the cupbearer of the help he has given him; requests him to remember and help Joseph to get out of prison as well. I love how sometimes we think we can use our gifting to take the opportunity to make a deal and help get ourselves out of a difficult situation. *Hey God! I'll get myself out of your testing of my life! I'll take it from here!* You can imagine and most likely, not unlike myself, relate to Joseph in this situation. *I've helped you! Now you help me out of this predicament!*

There are times when we want to use our giftings for our own benefit. God knew the timing He had for Joseph's life. God had placed Joseph in prison and only God would deliver him from the situation, when God was ready—God-given gifting for Joseph or not. God had allowed the timing of three men to be placed into prison, at the same location in time. He shows us some amazing truths as this small portion of Scripture is dissected. I love how the Word of God is inexhaustible! It is so rich and full of revelation, which God highlights to those who read His Word!

Chapter Nine

⸺

The Chief Baker

Genesis chapter 40
verses 16–23

Now, within our human nature, we want all the good that someone else experiences for ourselves. There is nothing wrong with this—especially in the day we live, specifically in the area of prophecy. We are seeing in a large number of circles, that we are taught to only speak nice and good, and nothing bad will ever happen! Some are teaching that today God doesn't judge, or use His authority to rebuke or correct a Christian. Again, some would say that the God of the Old Testament is a different God of the New Testament— how utterly silly! Jesus Christ is the same yesterday, today, and forever! People really haven't changed much over the centuries. The Chief Baker, after being an eye witness to the ministry of Joseph to the Chief Butler, wants his dream interpreted believing it would be a good ending for him as well.

When the baker heard the interpretation of the butler's dream, he was eager to get his own dream heard from Joseph. Again, looking at Scripture:

> When the Chief Baker saw that the interpretation was favourable, he said to Joseph, "I also had a dream: there were three cake baskets on my head, and in the uppermost basket there were all sorts of baked food for Pharaoh, but the birds were eating it out of the basket on my head." And Joseph answered and said, "This is its interpretation: the three baskets are three days. In three days, Pharaoh will lift up your head—from you! —and hang you on a tree. And the birds will eat the flesh from you. (Genesis chapter 40 verses 16-19)

Once again, the three baskets are three days. Here, we see again different imagery used: branches in the Butler's dream and baskets in the Chief Baker's dream. The number three is used in both dreams and the meaning is once again representing days. The result of the first dream is positive; the result of the second dream is not positive for the dreamer.

When looking at numbers and biblical numeric, one can fall into the trap of just going to a reference book, such as a dream dictionary or some other interpretation resource, and then always applying the meaning to a symbol or number every time. This is dangerous practice, and in my opinion can verge on witchcraft. We need to ask the Holy Spirit in prayer. The very *first* thing you should consider doing is asking the Holy Spirit for the meaning of your dream.

The interpretation is not good for the baker, as he

is told he would be beheaded and hung on a tree, and the birds would eat his flesh. This actually happens, sadly enough. Now, just taking a pause here, can I say that in actual fact, this is where it gets like 'splitting hairs' when we discuss dreams and visions. I have already mentioned that dreams and visions use metaphoric language. The wording used in this instance is *dream,* and that is what it is, and because it actually takes place, it can fall into a *dream vision.* It is a state of being in a dream but, in actual fact, the events take place in real life. There are no natural baskets used, this is colloquial expression as bakers would use baskets. There is a Holy Ghost intervention to give the interpreter, Joseph, the understanding of the number of days, just as in the dream interpreted for the butler.

This is what I call a destiny dream, for the butler and the baker with two totally different outcomes, yet both would be in the same time frame. Not every dream is about nice things, this is a fact that some in Christianity have a hard time admitting in today's growing Western Christian culture. God sometimes tells us information that becomes a revelation for the dreamer, or the interpreter, that is not what the dreamer necessarily wants to hear or receive.

The last verse in the book of Genesis chapter 40 verse 23, clearly states that Joseph, even though he was accurate in the interpretation that he received from God, was not honoured, he was forgotten by the butler and Joseph remained in prison according to the plan of God.

> Yet the chief cupbearer did not remember Joseph but forgot him.

Sometimes we have the opportunity to take offence in situations, when we are ministering accurately in the Lord's anointing, that is upon or working through our lives. We can find ourselves not honoured or celebrated. In fact, there could be times when we are given no credit or mention by people who are greatly impacted by what God does, using our lives and giftings. I believe these moments are set up scenarios by God who loves us, and wants us to walk in humility and character. God *does* test us in our journey in Him! God wants us to pass the tests that come, so that we can be entrusted to minister for His benefit and plan, and not for the rewards man can give to us.

> …so that the tested genuineness of your faith—more precious than gold that perishes though it is tested by fire—may be found to result in praise and glory and honour at the revelation of Jesus Christ. (1 Peter chapter 1 verse 7)

Now let's take a look two years later at Joseph in Genesis chapter 41. Pharaoh, the leader of the nation of Egypt, has a dream in which he cannot understand and needs the interpretation. Joseph had walked a God-ordained path in life up to this point

He was betrayed and sold into slavery by his brothers. He was taken to Egypt, experienced some favour and then was placed into prison unjustly. He is forgotten for two years, after being tested in accuracy in interpreting dreams for chief officials in prison. Joseph was then put in the position of second in charge of the entire nation of Egypt, second only to the Pharaoh himself.

Life has many ups and downs. Through the life of Joseph, we can read that through his journey there are some relatable points to us as readers of Scripture. I can empathise in some of what he might have been feeling through his sentence in prison. For two long years Joseph was stuck in a position that he could not get himself out from.

Have you ever felt like the situation you find yourself in feels like a prison sentence and there is nothing you can do about it? Then there is the intervention of God, and what seems like a prison, we find ourselves released from, and a plan from God is made evident to us.

Chapter Ten

Dream types

Types of dreams not unlike gifts, abilities, and talents, are hard to compartmentalise and separate, totally, one from the other. There is overlap when you start to talk about spiritual things as well. The gifts of the Spirit are a good example where, we can see in the book of John chapter 4 verses 13 to 26, Jesus Himself moved in the gifts of wisdom, words of knowledge, encouragement and prophecy, and brought a woman to salvation in the process.

> Jesus said to her, "Everyone who drinks of this water will be thirsty again, but whoever drinks of the water that I will give him will never be thirsty again. The water that I will give him will become in him a spring of water welling up to eternal life." The woman said to him, "Sir, give me this water, so that I will not be thirsty or have to come here to draw water." Jesus said to her, "Go, call your husband, and come here." The woman answered him, "I have no husband." Jesus said to her, "You are right in saying,

'I have no husband'; for you have had five husbands, and the one you now have is not your husband. What you have said is true." The woman said to him, "Sir, I perceive that you are a prophet. Our fathers worshiped on this mountain, but you say that in Jerusalem is the place where people ought to worship." Jesus said to her, "Woman, believe me, the hour is coming when neither on this mountain nor in Jerusalem will you worship the Father. You worship what you do not know; we worship what we know, for salvation is from the Jews. But the hour is coming, and is now here, when the true worshipers will worship the Father in spirit and truth, for the Father is seeking such people to worship him. God is spirit, and those who worship him must worship in spirit and truth." The woman said to him, "I know that Messiah is coming (he who is called Christ). When he comes, he will tell us all things." Jesus said to her, "I who speak to you am he."

I think, here, is a good place to weave the types of dreams that could take place. I want to say I don't have an exhaustive number; nor do I claim to know all the categories or profess to be the foremost expert on dreams. Some people will describe categories or types, and in one chapter I have mentioned destiny dream, and in another chapter, restoration. Again, to be repetitive on purpose there are only three sources of dreams: God, our soul, or the Devil.

To first have a discussion of types of dreams one needs to know that, there are dreams that apply to the dreamer and there are dreams that apply to others. I have found that a majority of dreams are about the dreamer, even when it doesn't seem like there is application. Dreams are to help the dreamer in their journey in Christ on earth.

Psalm chapter 84 verse 5 says:

> Blessed are those whose strength is in you, whose hearts are set on pilgrimage. (NIV)

Why would God give us a dream about an event that we might not be directly involved in, or that doesn't directly affect me or my family etc.? It is the heart of God that He calls people He wants to entrust with intercession, on the behalf of others. *The others* do not have to be known, related by blood, friends or acquaintances in any way, shape or form. They don't even have to be those who will be alive when we get the information. We have already seen where God gave Abraham insight into events 400 years into the future within the captivity of Israel.

God loves prayer. He loves to draw us closer to Him in relationship. There is something about God that He desires to extend involvement, with regard to His ultimate plan, wanting humanity to be involved in the fulfilment of the plan. To me this is a wonderful, and sometimes overwhelming, reality to think about. Intercession is one type of prayer to be able to stand in the gap, or go to God, on behalf of others. God shares things with us at times, for us to pray for those involved in circumstances we can't relate to, or are involved directly with, but He wants us to be in compassion and empathy with these people.

Types of dreams can include destiny, which I have mentioned, as well as restoration. There are dreams that build a person up in their faith in Christ, as well as provide encouragement. There are dreams that bring comfort, as well as correction or discipline. Why does

God bring correction or discipline to the life of a believer in Him? The Bible says God corrects or disciplines those He loves.

> And have you forgotten the exhortation that addresses you as sons? "My son do not regard lightly the discipline of the Lord, nor be weary when reproved by him. For the Lord disciplines the one he loves and chastises every son whom he receives." It is for discipline that you have to endure. God is treating you as sons. For what son is there whom his father does not discipline? (Hebrews chapter 12 verses 5-7)

God gives directional dreams, as well as dreams that give instruction from God. God will give invention or creative dreams to people. For my own life, I have received many creative answers to questions, within dreams. I received a name of a company that we started through a dream, as well as an invention that is yet to be produced, but the conceptional drawings and workings of the invention have been tested so far and are more than feasible. You can look at history, of God giving plans and strategies to General George Patton in dreams. An invention was made from a nightmare that Mr Elias Howe had one evening and from this dream the sewing machine was invented.

God can use a dream to help us engage in spiritual warfare. Isaiah chapter 54 verse 17 says:

> ...no weapon that is fashioned against you shall succeed, and you shall refute every tongue that rises against you in judgment. This is the heritage of the servants of the Lord and their vindication from me," declares the Lord.

As well as looking into Ephesians chapter 6 verses 6-12:

> ...not by the way of eye-service, as people-pleasers, but as bondservants of Christ, doing the will of God from the heart, rendering service with a good will as to the Lord and not to man, knowing that whatever good anyone does, this he will receive back from the Lord, whether he is a bondservant or is free. Masters, do the same to them, and stop your threatening, knowing that he who is both their Master and yours is in heaven, and that there is no partiality with him.

> Finally, be strong in the Lord and in the strength of his might. Put on the whole armour of God, that you may be able to stand against the schemes of the devil. For we do not wrestle against flesh and blood, but against the rulers, against the authorities, against the cosmic powers over this present darkness, against the spiritual forces of evil in the heavenly places.

God can use a dream to activate something of Himself in the life of the dreamer. He can give wisdom, courage, boldness, joy etc. Some call these dreams 'impartation dreams'. God can also reveal what is in a man or woman's heart.

I have met people who have disclosed the contents of their dream and then they have received a healing in some area of their life, physically, emotionally, relationally or financially, by God bringing healing to that dreamer through the dream. Looking in the book of Jeremiah chapter 30, verse 17 God says:

> For I will restore health to you, and your wounds I will heal, declares the Lord, because they have called

you an outcast: "It is Zion, for whom no one cares!"

The book of Matthew chapter 8 verses 16-17 says:

> That evening they brought to him many who were oppressed by demons, and he cast out the spirits with a word and healed all who were sick. This was to fulfil what was spoken by the prophet Isaiah: "He took our illnesses and bore our diseases."

And Isaiah chapter 53 verse 5 (reflected again in 1 Peter chapter 2 verse 24):

> But he was pierced for our transgressions; he was crushed for our iniquities; upon him was the chastisement that brought us peace, and with his wounds we are healed.

There are dreams that come from the condition of a soul. Again, it isn't necessarily a type I'm mentioning here but, the source of a dream, can be the soul of the dreamer. When a person is unwell or on strong medication it can affect the contents of the dream; when a woman is pregnant, when there are hormonal issues, or chemical stimulus from caffeine or food. My lovely wife is a successful Wellness Coach and knows so much about the role that well balanced hormones play in cultivating a healthy and vigorous lifestyle. She has helped numerous people in this area, and many have had dreams that accompany their hormonal imbalances.

The other source of dreams is dark, and is not from God. The enemy of our soul, Satan, can affect dreams. Now, this is not again to say all dreams are what we would term demonic. God does not want a person to be in fear, phobia, depression, panic, anxiety, divorce, hatred, violence, horror or terror. So, noticing the mood or tone in the dream can help determine the source. If you are a believer in Christ, take authority in Jesus' name over the enemy and command the dreams to stop. Ask God to intervene and give you godly dreams from Him. Dark, black, deceptive dreams are not given by God, but God can allow them to take place so the dreamer will take authority over the enemy in Jesus' name, or close any door that might be allowing an attack against them, such as lifestyle choices, what they are listening to, or watching, or engaging in action.

In my opinion there are many different types or categories of dreams. There are only three distinctive sources of all dreams, but the types of dreams are many more. Sometimes it helps to be able to place a dream within a category to aid in gaining the interpretation of the dream. I don't confess to know all the categories, and each type of dream is not spelled out to us in Scripture. This list once again is not exhaustive but may be helpful: healing; destiny or calling; restorative; encouragement; comfort; correction; warning; self-condition (soul); warfare; cleansing or deliverance; condition of the physical body can affect dreams; courage and directional.

Chapter Eleven

❦

Pharaoh

Genesis chapter 41
verses 1–32

Does God only speak to those people who would be considered to be living a godly, moral life? Does God only talk to those considered to be in the God-club or the fun bunch of church? God loves people! God's heart is to communicate His plan and salvation to people in general.

Pharaoh, the supreme ruler of the most powerful nation in the known world at that time in history, has two dreams one after the other on the same night. Each dream once again has different images, but the meaning of the dream is the same. God uses a dream of Pharaoh to elevate Joseph, but also to warn an entire nation to help the known world at that time.

This is an important point. God does speak truth to people who are not worshippers of Him. God can share vital, important information about events through dreams with people, who don't go to church or are considered Christian. Pharaoh is such a person. God can reveal things to a world leader!

> Pharaoh dreamed that he was standing by the Nile, and behold, there came up out of the Nile seven cows, attractive and plump, and they fed in the reed grass. And behold, seven other cows, ugly and thin, came up out of the Nile after them, and stood by the other cows on the bank of the Nile. And the ugly, thin cows ate up the seven attractive, plump cows. And Pharaoh awoke. And he fell asleep and dreamed a second time. And behold, seven ears of grain, plump and good, were growing on one stalk. And behold, after them sprouted seven ears, thin and blighted by the east wind. And the thin ears swallowed up the seven plump, full ears. And Pharaoh awoke, and behold, it was a dream. In the morning his spirit was troubled, and he sent and called for all the magicians of Egypt and all its wise men. Pharaoh told them his dreams, but there was none who could interpret them to Pharaoh. (Genesis chapter 41 verses 1-8)

Why would God give a dream to Pharaoh who worshipped multiple gods? God loves everyone, and will give information and revelation to anyone He desires to use for His purposes. This dream as the Scripture informs us, is about a famine that is coming to the world— there is a warning, so that there could be time used to prepare.

Joseph is even able to tell Pharaoh why he was given the dreams in a consecutive manner. In Genesis chapter 41 verse 32, Joseph says that, what was shown, was going to happen quickly. Joseph had already told the Pharaoh that there would be seven years of plenty and seven years of famine. Joseph experienced where his gifting made room for him, and he was used by God to save the known world from famine.

> And the doubling of Pharaoh's dream means that the thing is fixed by God, and God will shortly bring it about. (Genesis chapter 41 verse 32)

God can use a series of dreams to convey the same point. God wants us to understand what He is telling us. God spoke to Pharaoh using two very different dreams with the use of different symbols, yet, the meaning was the same. I want to bring attention that, after the first dream, the dreamer, Pharaoh, woke up. He then falls back to sleep and has another dream. I have found so many people that I have ministered to, have had this very same occurrence, where they dream and then awake, and then fall asleep and have another dream of different symbols, yet, the dream is of the same meaning. People can have two completely different dreams with different intended applications. There are occasions where I have met people who are emphatic, who have four or more different dreams in one night and they wake up in between each dream, and that, those dreams are unrelated to one another in application.

There are other people whom I have met, who have had numerous dreams in the night and have woken up. The dreams are directly connected, but each dream gives a furthering insight into details that God wants to make known to the dreamer in a progressive manner.

There are people who tend to be very, or highly, detailed. Can I say that, in the area of detail, I think God speaks often in specifics to detailed people; and at times detail to not so detailed people. It isn't necessary to think that the more intricate a dream is, the more it is from God. This is not one of the criteria I use in ascertaining if a dream is from God or not.

What criteria can you use toward examining if a dream is from God, or not? One of the best resources we have is to ask questions. A well-posed question is a very useful tool in interpreting if something is from God, or not. The Bible says, 'we don't have because we don't ask', so ask God if this means something pertaining to a dream you think might be from God.

> And this is the confidence that we have before Him:
> If we ask anything according to His will, He hears us.
> (1 John chapter 5 verse 14)

I suggest taking your dream and look at applying it to your own life first, and not to the life of someone else. Try to get as simple as you can with regard to a dream, I call this 'what is the gist?'. Also, a dream from God will never go against His written Word. Ask yourself what the mood of the dream was, or in the dream what was the tone? Another question could be, what was the basic emotion that was felt in the dream?

Writing down the dream, placing a date or title on the dream, doesn't make it spiritual or from God. If the dream carries weight or is vivid in colour, there are good indications the Lord is wanting you to search out the meaning of the dream from the Holy Spirit. Even though the meaning might be hidden or not blatantly known, there will be a curiosity that is stirred within the dreamer to want to search out more.

As I've stated, God does work within terms and areas that are familiar to the dreamer, as He wants us to get the understanding.

> "Come, follow me," Jesus said, "and I will send you out to fish for people." (Matthew chapter 4 verse 19)

Jesus spoke in a way that leant itself for the fisherman to be able to understand. We call this colloquial speech, where the terms are relevant to the person's culture, language or understanding. God does not want to keep humanity in the dark, and because of his grace He wants to communicate in such a way that at times people can understand the importance of the use of fish in the culture that they live in. Jesus uses metaphoric language. He is painting a picture in which the hearers could catch his intention to talking about evangelism and compares fish to people who need to hear the gospel message and be saved.

Chapter Twelve

∽

Samuel,
a vision more like it
1 Samuel chapter 3

Samuel was born when the Word of God was rare. God was speaking to Samuel, which was so unusual at the time, that Samuel did not know what was going on in his encounter. No one had heard the voice of God for so long that no one could recognise it. After a few attempts to tell his mentor Eli, the high priest, Eli finally realised what was happening; Samuel was being spoken to by God.

Samuel has a vision where he is told by God that there would be judgement coming to Eli's sons, as they were doing the wrong thing by God. Eli was not stopping them and God had had enough. There are dreams and visions from God where people are warned, by God, to turn from their actions or there would be consequences.

The word used in 1 Samuel chapter 3 verse 15,

is the word *vision*. The Hebrew word used here is, *mar-ah*. This word is used in relation to a mode or a way of revelation. The word *mar-ah* means, in English, a looking glass. God wants to be so specific at times, it is like looking in a mirror.

The revelation is so clear, as not to miss. Samuel received a message from God, in an unmistakably accurate fashion, through this vision. It is a vision because it is of events yet to take place. There was no need for metaphoric language, but the straight truth.

Samuel was afraid to tell Eli, but he was faithful to relay the information that God had shared with him about Eli's sons. This sometimes is the dilemma we have, when we get information about a subject, topic, or people. I believe that, because Samuel didn't withhold the truth from Eli, the Lord could trust Samuel with more and more revelation throughout his life.

This is an important time period and portion of Scripture, in regard to the prophetic, as this is the beginning of the word of the Lord becoming more frequent. In First Samuel chapter 1, the Hebrew word for vision used is, *chazon*.

There is another word used in Scripture which is, *chezev*, which means the same thing as *chazon*. There are several Scriptures that use these words, in which they mean that mental pictures are used by God to convey revelation to men. Some of the Scriptures, as above mentioned, are:

Psalm chapter 89 verse 19 (NIV):

> Once you spoke in a vision, to your faithful people you said: "I have bestowed strength on a warrior; I have raised up a young man from among the people."

Isaiah chapter 1 verse 1 (NIV):

> The vision concerning Judah and Jerusalem that Isaiah son of Amoz saw during the reigns of Uzziah, Jotham, Ahaz and Hezekiah, kings of Judah.

Ezekiel chapter 7 verse 13 (NIV):

> The seller will not recover the property that was sold—as long as both buyer and seller live. For the vision concerning the whole crowd will not be reversed. Because of their sins, not one of them will preserve their life.

Daniel chapter 1 verse 17 (NIV):

> To these four young men God gave knowledge and understanding of all kinds of literature and learning. And Daniel could understand visions and dreams of all kinds.

Micah chapter 3 verse 6 (NIV):

> Therefore night will come over you, without visions, and darkness, without divination. The sun will set for the prophets, and the day will go dark for them.

Habakkuk chapter 2 verses 2-3 (NIV):

> Then the LORD replied: "Write down the revelation and make it plain on tablets so that a herald may run with it. For the revelation awaits an appointed time; it speaks of the end and will not prove false. Though it linger, wait for it; it will certainly come and will not

delay.

This is, obviously, not an exhaustive list of Scripture but supports the meaning for which I mentioned previously.

I believe we are living in a day where the Word of God needs to be shared with people on earth in an expanding way. I would like to share a few things regarding *visions* in Scripture and believe this is the chapter to do so. Visions are a way in which God communicates to humanity and they tend to be more literal in interpretation and application. Dreams tend to be more symbolic. There are internal visions where the person receiving, sees the illustration or picture within themselves. Daniel chapter 4 verse 5:

> I saw a dream that made me afraid. As I lay in bed the fancies and the visions of my head alarmed me.

As you can see, even when a vision is given by God, it can disturb the one receiving the revelation or information.

Daniel chapter 4 verse 10:

> The visions of my head as I lay in bed were these: I saw, and behold, a tree in the midst of the earth, and its height was great.

Daniel chapter 4 verse 13:

> I saw in the visions of my head as I lay in bed, and behold, a watcher, a holy one, came down from heaven.

Daniel chapter 7 verse 2:

> I saw in my vision by night, and behold, the four
> winds of heaven were stirring up the great sea.

I will speak about Acts chapter 10 later in this book.
Jeremiah was in a place of deep meditation within his
own heart and God gave him a revelation during this
time.

> In His days Judah will be saved, And Israel will
> dwell safely; Now this is His name by which He will
> be called: THE LORD OUR RIGHTEOUSNESS.
> (Jeremiah chapter 23 verse 6 NKJV)

Jeremiah got a revelation of who the Lord will be in the
future. To us, we know it is Jesus Christ who fulfils this
Scripture, but this was a prophetic word of prophecy
through the prophet, that was revealed.

God spoke to men also in the act of praying to
God, as we read in the book of Daniel chapter 9 verses
21-24:

> ...yes, while I was speaking in prayer, the man Gabriel,
> whom I had seen in the vision at the beginning, being
> caused to fly swiftly, reached me about the time of
> the evening offering. And he informed me, and talked
> with me, and said, "O Daniel, I have now come forth
> to give you skill to understand. At the beginning
> of your supplications the command went out, and I
> have come to tell you, for you are greatly beloved;
> therefore consider the matter, and understand the
> vision: "Seventy weeks are determined for your people
> and for your holy city, to finish the transgression,

to make an end of sins, to make reconciliation for iniquity, to bring in everlasting righteousness, to seal up vision and prophecy, and to anoint the Most Holy. (NKJV)

God also spoke to men as they were awake and doing things in life.

Ezekiel chapter 8 verse 3:

He stretched out the form of a hand, and took me by a lock of my hair; and the Spirit lifted me up between earth and heaven, and brought me in visions of God to Jerusalem, to the door of the north gate of the inner court, where the seat of the image of jealousy was, which provokes to jealousy. (NKJV)

Ezekiel chapter 40 verse 2:

In the visions of God He took me into the land of Israel and set me on a very high mountain; on it toward the south was something like the structure of a city. (NKJV)

Matthew chapter 17 verses 1-9:

Now after six days Jesus took Peter, James, and John his brother, led them up on a high mountain by themselves; and He was transfigured before them. His face shone like the sun, and His clothes became as white as the light. And behold, Moses and Elijah appeared to them, talking with Him. Then Peter answered and said to Jesus, "Lord, it is good for us to be here; if You wish, let us make here three tabernacles: one for You, one for Moses, and one for Elijah." While he was still speaking, behold, a bright cloud overshadowed them; and suddenly a voice came out of the cloud, saying, "This is My beloved Son, in whom I am well pleased. Hear Him!" And when the disciples heard it, they fell on their faces and were greatly afraid. But Jesus came and touched them and said, "Arise, and do not be afraid." When they had lifted up their eyes, they saw no one but Jesus only. Now as they came down from the mountain, Jesus commanded them, saying, "Tell the vision to no one until the Son of Man is risen from the dead."

Luke chapter 24 verse 23:

When they did not find His body, they came saying that they had also seen a vision of angels who said He was alive. (NKJV)

Revelation chapter 1 verse 10:

I was in the Spirit on the Lord's Day, and I heard behind me a loud voice, as of a trumpet (NKJV)

Revelation chapter 4 verses 1-2:

Immediately I was in the Spirit; and behold, a throne set in heaven, and One sat on the throne. (NKJV)

Revelation chapter 4 verses 1-2:

I was in the Spirit on the Lord's Day, and I heard behind me a loud voice, as of a trumpet. (NKJV)

It is probably good to mention another place in Scripture where we see a God-given dream given to a person. This depiction is a bit obscure, I therefore will mention it within this chapter. In Judges chapter 7 verses 12-15, the Midianite and Amalekite armies are the enemies of God. God's choice of a leader was found in Gideon:

> Gideon arrived just as a man was telling a friend his dream. "I had a dream," he was saying. "A round loaf of barley bread came tumbling into the Midianite camp. It struck the tent with such force that the tent overturned and collapsed." His friend responded, "This can be nothing other than the sword of Gideon son of Joash, the Israelite. God has given the Midianites and the whole camp into his hands." When Gideon heard the dream and its interpretation, he bowed down and worshiped. He returned to the camp of Israel and called out, "Get up! the LORD has given the Midianite camp into your hands." (Judges chapter 7 verses 13-15 NIV)

Chapter Thirteen

∂∽

The Midianite

Judges chapter 7
verses 13–15

I would like to mention that the Midianites and the Amalekites were enemies of God and also, they were not followers of Yahweh in any way, shape or form. Yet, God told Gideon to sneak into the camp of the enemy at night. Gideon obeyed the Lord's direction and went into the camp at the outposts of the enemy. Gideon overhears an enemy soldier relating a dream that he had just had. Gideon overhears his enemy tell the dream and the interpretation given by the soldier listening to the dream. The soldier interpreting, mentions Gideon's name and gives an accurate prediction, that Israel would win the battle against them. This revelation greatly encourages Gideon, who overhears the entire dialogue.

This is so interesting to me, as well as being encouraging. It is yet, another instance when God allows there to be insight that only He can give, because He is all-knowing, see in the book of Isaiah chapter 46 and verses 9-10:

> Remember the former things, those of long ago; I am God, and there is no other; I am God, and there is none like me. I make known the end from the beginning, from ancient times, what is still to come. I say: My purpose will stand, and I will do all that I please. (NIV)

Also, when reading in the book of Psalms chapter 33, verses 13 and 14:

> From heaven the LORD looks down and sees all mankind; from his dwelling place he watches all who live on earth—he who forms the hearts of all, who considers everything they do. (NIV)

Even in the New Testament it is evident that God is all-knowing. In the book of Hebrews chapter 4 verse 13:

> Nothing in all creation is hidden from God's sight. Everything is uncovered and laid bare before the eyes of him to whom we must give account. (NIV)

God revealed these things to the enemy soldier who was against Gideon. Gideon was favoured by God and commissioned by God, to win the victory. God gives a prophetic dream with illustration, to prove that the Midianite and Amalekite army will not prevail. We don't know the heart of the dreamer in this instance. There is no supportive description if this man knew God, wanted to serve God, or thought the plan was doomed for his army? It just states the dream as a matter-of-fact, and has

Gideon over-hear it.

In the book of Judges chapter 7, verse 13, the soldier recounts he dreamed of a cake of barley bread that tumbled into the tent of the soldier, who was a Midianite:

> When Gideon came, behold, a man was telling a dream to his comrade. And he said, "Behold, I dreamed a dream, and behold, a cake of barley bread tumbled into the camp of Midian and came to the tent and struck it so that it fell and turned it upside down, so that the tent lay flat."

This is very interesting because, back in the book of Judges chapter 6 verse 11, verses 19-21, Gideon was approached by the Angel of the Lord while he was threshing wheat in a wine press:

> Now the angel of the Lord came and sat under the terebinth at Ophrah, which belonged to Joash the Abiezrite, while his son Gideon was beating out wheat in the winepress to hide it from the Midianites.

Also, in reference to verses 19 through 21, Gideon makes 'unleavened cakes', but some translations say 'barley cakes':

> So, Gideon went into his house and prepared a young goat and unleavened cakes from an ephah of flour. The meat he put in a basket, and the broth he put in a pot, and brought them to him under the terebinth and presented them. And the angel of God said to him, "Take the meat and the unleavened cakes, and put them on this rock, and pour the broth over them." And he did so. Then the angel of the Lord reached out

the tip of the staff that was in his hand and touched the meat and the unleavened cakes. And fire sprang up from the rock and consumed the meat and the unleavened cakes. And the angel of the Lord vanished from his sight.

Once again, here we have God using colloquial language, or words that are familiar. This dream was not for the dreamer but for Gideon to hear in the exact timing of God; as God had instructed him to sneak into the camp, at the exact time he would hear what was being discussed by the two enemy soldiers.

His friend responded, "This can be nothing other than the sword of Gideon son of Joash, the Israelite. God has given the Midianites and the whole camp into his hands." (Judges chapter 7 verse 14 NIV)

The cake of barley bread represented Gideon. Interestingly, it is the friend of the soldier who had the dream, who gets the accurate interpretation. This dream is such an encouragement to Gideon, that he returns to his camp and tells everyone in the camp of Israel, that the Lord had delivered the Midianites into the hand of Israel.

We can look at this dream which is so small in comparison to others, and look over it without thought. The dream means nothing to the dreamer because it is, actually, a timed 'overhear' by Gideon, whereby God wanted Gideon to hear it and take courage. Remember, it was Gideon that had trouble with courage, in his calling encounter with the Angel of God.

Now the angel of the Lord came and sat under the

terebinth at Ophrah, which belonged to Joash the Abiezrite, while his son Gideon was beating out wheat in the winepress to hide it from the Midianites. And the angel of the Lord appeared to him and said to him, "The Lord is with you, O mighty man of valour." And Gideon said to him, "Please, my lord, if the Lord is with us, why then has all this happened to us? And where are all his wonderful deeds that our fathers recounted to us, saying, 'Did not the Lord bring us up from Egypt?' But now the Lord has forsaken us and given us into the hand of Midian."

And the Lord turned to him and said, "Go in this might of yours and save Israel from the hand of Midian; do not I send you?" And he said to him, "Please, Lord, how can I save Israel? Behold, my clan is the weakest in Manasseh, and I am the least in my father's house." And the Lord said to him, "But I will be with you, and you shall strike the Midianites as one man." And he said to him, "If now I have found favour in your eyes, then show me a sign that it is you who speak with me. Please do not depart from here until I come to you and bring out my present and set it before you." And he said, "I will stay till you return."

So, Gideon went into his house and prepared a young goat and unleavened cakes from an ephah of flour. The meat he put in a basket, and the broth he put in a pot, and brought them to him under the terebinth and presented them. And the angel of God said to him, "Take the meat and the unleavened cakes, and put them on this rock, and pour the broth over them." And he did so. Then the angel of the Lord reached out the tip of the staff that was in his hand and touched the meat

85

and the unleavened cakes. And fire sprang up from the rock and consumed the meat and the unleavened cakes. And the angel of the Lord vanished from his sight. Then Gideon perceived that he was the angel of the Lord. And Gideon said, "Alas, O Lord God! For now, I have seen the angel of the Lord face to face." But the Lord said to him, "Peace be to you. Do not fear; you shall not die." Then Gideon built an altar there to the Lord and called it, The Lord Is Peace. To this day it still stands at Ophrah, which belongs to the Abiezrites. (Judges chapter 6 verses 11-24)

It's incredible how God uses anyone, and everyone, in His great plan. Gideon was a man who received the instruction of the Lord and obeyed those instructions. What if he didn't obey God and go into the enemy's camp? That would have been a missed opportunity for Gideon, in many ways. How about in our lives? Are we willing to go where God wants us to go to be encouraged, even if that is in the most unlikely places using the most unlikely people? Once again, we see God using non-followers of the truth, to receive truth in a God-given dream.

Chapter Fourteen

∽

Solomon

1 Kings chapter 3
verse 5

Solomon is credited with being the wisest person ever to live on the face of the earth. He was asked by God in a famous offer: 'Ask what you wish of Me to give you' (1 Kings chapter 3 verse 5). What is missed by some, is that this was during a God-initiated dream that Solomon was having.

This is a dream where God is interacting with the dreamer in relationship. Solomon needed help to rule this great nation, which, David his father had led before him. Solomon did not ask for long life, wealth, or victory. He asked for the gift of God to be bestowed upon him, namely, wisdom from God.

It pleased the Lord that Solomon had asked this. And God said to him, "Because you have asked this, and have not asked for yourself long life or riches or the life of your enemies but have asked for yourself understanding to discern what is right, behold, I now do according to your word. Behold, I give you a wise and discerning mind, so that none like you has been before you and none like you shall arise after you. (1 Kings chapter 3, verses 10-12)

He could have asked through selfish ambition. However, he asks for the gifting that can only come from God. A God-inspired attribute was Solomon's request. It says that God was pleased with Solomon because of his request, (see verse 10). Interestingly, God gives him more than he asked for as God was pleased with him. The favour of the Lord is granted to Solomon's life and he also gets wealth and honour. No other king would ever be like King Solomon, (see verse 13). Verse 15 clearly says, that Solomon awoke from the dream.

"I give you also what you have not asked, both riches and honour, so that no other king shall compare with you, all your days. And if you will walk in my ways, keeping my statutes and my commandments, as your father David walked, then I will lengthen your days." And Solomon awoke, and behold, it was a dream. Then he came to Jerusalem and stood before the ark of the covenant of the Lord, and offered up burnt offerings and peace offerings, and made a feast for all his servants. (1 Kings chapter 3, verses 13-15)

There are times when God chooses to engage humanity through the use of a dream instead of a physical encounter, as He has done on occasions throughout Scripture. God chose to physically manifest Himself and wrestled with Jacob, in Genesis chapter 32. Here in 1 Kings chapter 3,

God used a dream to offer an invitation for the dreamer Solomon, to ask of God what he wanted.

In Scripture we see that God offers this same invitation to His followers.

Matthew chapter 7, verse 7 (NKJV):

> Ask and you shall receive, seek and you shall find, knock and it shall be opened

Matthew chapter 17, verse 20 (NKJV):

> ...nothing shall be impossible unto you

Matthew chapter 21, verse 22 (NKJV):

> All things whatsoever you shall ask in prayer, believing, you shall receive

John chapter 15, verses 7 and 16 (NKJV):

> ...ask what you will, and it shall be done unto you

We see that Solomon has a view of himself, and it is revealed in verse 7 of 1 Kings chapter 3. Solomon states he is a little child and he doesn't know how to go out or come in. Solomon is feeling the pressure and realises the weight of responsibility that has been given to him. Solomon moves in humility at this point, seeking help from God.

> And now, O Lord my God, you have made your servant king in place of David my father, although I

am but a little child. I do not know how to go out or come in. (v.7 KJV)

Humility is such a necessary attribute for all saints of God to possess: 'He leads the humble in what is right and teaches the humble his way.' (Psalm chapter 25 verse 9)

Then in the book of James chapter 4, verses 6 to 8:

> But he gives more grace. Therefore, it says, "God opposes the proud but gives grace to the humble". Submit yourselves therefore to God. Resist the devil, and he will flee from you. Draw near to God, and he will draw near to you. Cleanse your hands, you sinners, and purify your hearts, you double-minded.

Lastly in the book of 1 Peter chapter 4, verses 10 and 11:

> As each has received a gift, use it to serve one another, as good stewards of God's varied grace: whoever speaks, as one who speaks oracles of God; whoever serves, as one who serves by the strength that God supplies—in order that in everything God may be glorified through Jesus Christ. To him belong glory and dominion forever and ever. Amen.

Solomon coming to God in a child-like approach, is also how God intends for his followers to posture themselves in position to Jesus.

> And calling to him a child, he put him in the midst of them and said, "Truly, I say to you, unless you turn and become like children, you will never enter the kingdom of heaven. Whoever humbles himself like

this child is the greatest in the kingdom of heaven."
(Matthew chapter 18 verses 2-4)

...but Jesus said, "Let the little children come to
me and do not hinder them, for to such belongs the
kingdom of heaven." (Matthew chapter 19 verse 14)
But Jesus called them to him, saying, "Let the
children come to me, and do not hinder them, for to
such belongs the kingdom of God." (Luke chapter 18
verse 16)

There is a drastic difference between childlike and
childish. God is not calling his followers to a life of
being self-absorbed, narcissistic, selfish and wanting
to be served continuously. On the contrary, God is
looking for mature believers. What father wouldn't want
their children to reach full maturity in every arena of
behaviour and life. I believe it is God's intention to bring
each believer into the awareness that even though we can
be mature, we can be intentional about being innocent,
open and humble. To be childlike is to be vulnerable and
allow ourselves to realise we don't know the answers,
and ask those who can lead us to truth; mainly the Holy
Spirit, God Himself.

To be childlike is one of the pre-requisites it
seems, to be able to interact with the kingdom of God
on earth. God definitely desires full maturity and He
shows this in the implementation of the fivefold minister
offices, found in Ephesians chapter 4 verses 11-12:

And he gave the apostles, the prophets, the evangelists,
the shepherds and teachers, to equip the saints for
the work of ministry, for building up the body of
Christ, until we all attain to the unity of the faith

91

and of the knowledge of the Son of God, to mature manhood, to the measure of the stature of the fullness of Christ, so that we may no longer be children, tossed to and fro by the waves and carried about by every wind of doctrine, by human cunning, by craftiness in deceitful schemes.

God wants to bring us into a mature stature, with the spiritual gifts in mind. Character development is a core desire of God for His children. We need to value wisdom and pursue her. In the book of Proverbs chapter 8, is the picture of how the spirit of Wisdom cries out for people to find her. God is looking for men's heart to be learnt, by the free will of man in the pursuit of maturity, through humility and wisdom.

Proverbs chapter 8:

> Does not wisdom call? Does not understanding raise her voice?

> On the heights beside the way, at the crossroads she takes her stand; beside the gates in front of the town, at the entrance of the portals she cries aloud: "To you, O men, I call, and my cry is to the children of man.

> O simple ones, learn prudence; O fools, learn sense.

> Hear, for I will speak noble things, and from my lips will come what is right, for my mouth will utter truth; wickedness is an abomination to my lips.

> All the words of my mouth are righteous; there is nothing twisted or crooked in them.
> They are all straight to him who understands, and

right to those who find knowledge.

Take my instruction instead of silver, and knowledge rather than choice gold, for wisdom is better than jewels, and all that you may desire cannot compare with her. "I, wisdom, dwell with prudence, and I find knowledge and discretion.

The fear of the Lord is hatred of evil. Pride and arrogance and the way of evil and perverted speech I hate. I have counsel and sound wisdom; I have insight; I have strength. By me kings reign, and rulers decree what is just; by me princes rule, and nobles, all who govern justly, I love those who love me, and those who seek me diligently find me.

Riches and honour are with me, enduring wealth and righteousness. My fruit is better than gold, even fine gold, and my yield than choice silver. I walk in the way of righteousness, in the paths of justice, granting an inheritance to those who love me, and filling their treasuries.

"The Lord possessed me at the beginning of his work, the first of his acts of old. Ages ago I was set up, at the first, before the beginning of the earth.

When there were no depths I was brought forth, when there were no springs abounding with water. Before the mountains had been shaped, before the hills, I was brought forth, before he had made the earth with its fields, or the first of the dust of the world.

When he established the heavens, I was there;

when he drew a circle on the face of the deep,
when he made firm the skies above,
when he established the fountains of the deep,
when he assigned to the sea its limit,
so that the waters might not transgress his
command, when he marked out the foundations
of the earth, then I was beside him, like a master
workman, and I was daily his delight, rejoicing
before him always, rejoicing in his inhabited world
and delighting in the children of man.

"And now, O sons, listen to me: blessed are those who
keep my ways. Hear instruction and be wise,
and do not neglect it.

Blessed is the one who listens to me, watching daily
at my gates, waiting beside my doors.

For whoever finds me finds life and obtains favour
from the Lord, but he who fails to find me injures
himself; all who hate me love death."

Chapter Fifteen

✵

Daniel and Nebuchadnezzar

Daniel chapter 2

Daniel is such an interesting individual who God used on numerous occasions, to speak and deliver truth in an empire that was based upon the worship of false gods. Daniel is known by most who read Scripture, as the dream interpreter. He has dreams and visions of apocalyptic events that many have attempted to interpret and conceptualize, even in this very modern day we live.

Daniel was in a position of affluence coming from a nobility upbringing, before the captivity under Babylonian rule. He was chosen, along with other young men, to be educated and taught the ways of Babylonian culture, tradition and spiritual development. I love how Father God gets people from every kind of background, social status and economic situation, to be involved in His plan. He uses people from royalty and of everyday common situations. Daniel himself was a dreamer. He had visions as well. Internal visions are where the person sees with the eyes of the spirit, or heart; or what some call, the eyes of our understanding, found in Ephesians chapter 1 verse 18:

> ...having the eyes of your hearts enlightened, that you may know what is the hope to which he has called you, what are the riches of his glorious inheritance in the saints

I want to bring out the fact that Daniel is an example of God using the affluent individual—a person from means, wealth, status. It seems, more and more, that as people become increasingly about themselves, instead of looking out for others, jealousy and competition can arise in the church. The world is jealous of those who have more than themselves, based upon greed and envy.

God allowed a captivity to happen but during that captivity, Daniel, Ezekiel and Jeremiah all have flourishing ministries. God chooses who and how, why, where, and when He will use a person for His glory and good will. Daniel is a symbol in part, in my opinion, of the affluent nations that God can use, or an individual that finds themselves in slavery by diverse ways. There are people God will use in spite of natural tough circumstances. There will be those who will not be defiled by the world and never relinquish the worship of Jesus, in the midst of pressure, to worship a sub-god of any description. In the world where there are so many choices, vices and distractions, Daniel is a prophetic symbol of a people who will never bow the knee to any other but Jesus Christ!

Daniel is also a very interesting character in Scripture, as he is forced into captivity, and yet, his gifting and abilities are recognised. I'm not sure how you would react or be, in this situation, should it have happened in your life. Here we see mentioned one of the most intensive cultures within Babylon, that emphasises spirituality. Revelation chapter 5 verse 17 says:

> And on her forehead a name was written:
> MYSTERY, BABYLON THE GREAT, THE MOTHER OF HARLOTS AND OF THE ABOMINATIONS OF THE EARTH.

Now, in my opinion, it does not state what giftings or abilities, tendencies or aptitudes Daniel and his friends had before captivity, at all. However, it says that he was good looking, showed wisdom, and had some abilities that were recognised. God chose to use Daniel and his friends as God willed to do so.

> Then the king instructed Ashpenaz, the master of his eunuchs, to bring some of the children of Israel and some of the king's descendants and some of the nobles, young men in whom there was no blemish, but good-looking, gifted in all wisdom, possessing knowledge and quick to understand, who had ability to serve in the king's palace, and whom they might teach the language and literature of the Chaldeans.
> (Daniel chapter 1 verses 3-4)

Daniel and his three friends, according to Scripture, were given the ability to interpret dreams and visions by God.

As a matter of fact, they were ten times wiser in the area of learning about such things. They were wiser due to God's favour and choosing for their lives.

> As for these four young men, God gave them knowledge and skill in all literature and wisdom; and Daniel had understanding in all visions and dreams.
>
> Now at the end of the days, when the king had said that they should be brought in, the chief of the eunuchs brought them in before Nebuchadnezzar. Then the king interviewed them, and among them all none was found like Daniel, Hananiah, Mishael, and Azariah; therefore, they served before the king. And in all matters of wisdom and understanding about which the king examined them, he found them ten times better than all the magicians and astrologers who were in all his realm. Thus, Daniel continued until the first year of King Cyrus. (Daniel chapter 1 verses 18-21 NKJV)

Father God gives every good and perfect gift. He is called the Father of Lights. He brings illumination and insight into what man cannot know or see. James chapter 1 verse 17 says:

> Every good gift and every perfect gift is from above, coming down from the Father of lights, with whom there is no variation or shadow due to change.

There are times when a vision can be laced within a dream. Daniel had visions of the mind within his dreams.

> I saw a dream that made me afraid. As I lay in bed the fancies and the visions of my head alarmed me.

(Daniel chapter 4 verse 5)

The visions of my head as I lay in bed were these: I saw, and behold, a tree in the midst of the earth, and its height was great. (Daniel chapter 4, verse 10)

Then verse 13 of Daniel chapter 4:

I saw in the visions of my head as I lay in bed, and behold, a watcher, a holy one, came down from heaven.

As well as Daniel chapter 7 verse 2:

Daniel declared, "I saw in my vision by night, and behold, the four winds of heaven were stirring up the great sea."

And again:

I raised my eyes and saw, and behold, a ram standing on the bank of the canal. It had two horns, and both horns were high, but one was higher than the other, and the higher one came up last. (Daniel chapter 8 verse 3)

These are called 'dream/visions' in certain circles. It is when a person who is having a dream goes into a vision while dreaming, and it is all in the context of the dream. An example is found in the book of Daniel chapter 4 verse 9:

O Belteshazzar, chief of the magicians, because I know that the Spirit of the Holy God is in you, and no secret troubles you, explain to me the visions of my dream that I have seen, and its interpretation.

God sometimes chooses to use the unusual thing, or things that are not easily explained or understood. I have found Jesus to be a wonderful creator of mystery. I would have to say, that when God moves or does something, I have more questions perhaps, than answers. I have talked to people who can relate to this very type of encounter with a dream/vision.

With all that said, in the book of Daniel chapter 2 the king of Babylon had a dream, and there was no one to interpret this dream that disturbed the king. The king even threatened all the magicians and sorcerers with death if they could not tell him his dream.

Daniel chapter 1 verses 1-6:

> In the second year of the reign of Nebuchadnezzar, Nebuchadnezzar had dreams; his spirit was troubled, and his sleep left him. Then the king commanded that the magicians, the enchanters, the sorcerers, and the Chaldeans be summoned to tell the king his dreams. So, they came in and stood before the king. And the king said to them, "I had a dream, and my spirit is troubled to know the dream." Then the Chaldeans said to the king in Aramaic, "O king, live forever! Tell your servants the dream, and we will show the interpretation. "The king answered and said to the Chaldeans, "The word from me is firm: if you do not make known to me the dream and its interpretation, you shall be torn limb from limb, and your houses shall be laid in ruins. But if you show the dream and its interpretation, you shall receive from

me gifts and rewards and great honour. Therefore, show me the dream and its interpretation."

Here we have a very interesting twist within the interpretation of dreams. When first reading this text, I used to think that the King forgot his own dream but, how could he then punish so severely those who attempted to tell him his dream if they should get it wrong? I've since come to see that this was a test set up by the King for the magicians, enchanters, the sorcerers, and Chaldeans. Here the dreamer remembers the dream and wants it interpreted but, is wanting to see who really has a gifting and hears or sees from the Divine.

Daniel 2:31-35:

> You saw, O king, and behold, a great image. This image, mighty and of exceeding brightness, stood before you, and its appearance was frightening. The head of this image was of fine gold, its chest and arms of silver, its middle and thighs of bronze, its legs of iron, its feet partly of iron and partly of clay. As you looked, a stone was cut out by no human hand, and it struck the image on its feet of iron and clay and broke them in pieces. Then the iron, the clay, the bronze, the silver, and the gold, all together were broken in pieces, and became like the chaff of the summer threshing floors; and the wind carried them away, so that not a trace of them could be found. But the stone that struck the image became a great mountain and filled the whole earth.

So, if I were to write this out, I would use a form of highlighting, such as the following:

Big/Huge Terrifying image
Head-gold
Chest/arms- silver
Middle/thighs- bronze
Legs-iron
Feet- mix clay and iron
Wind blows all away- can't be found
Stone struck image became Great Mountain
Stone filled whole earth

This is what I personally would make of the dream. I don't like to write in linear sentences or paragraph's, as the wording is too close. I like to separate things out so that I can take a look at them as the Holy Spirit is showing me certain things.

The interpretation

Daniel chapter 2 verses 36-42:

> This was the dream. Now we will tell the king its interpretation. You, O king, the king of kings, to whom the God of heaven has given the kingdom, the power, and the might, and the glory, and into whose hand he has given, wherever they dwell, the children of man, the beasts of the field, and the birds of the heavens, making you rule over them all—you are the head of gold. Another kingdom inferior to you shall arise after you, and yet a third kingdom of bronze, which shall rule over all the earth. And there shall be a fourth kingdom, strong as iron, because iron breaks to pieces and shatters all things. And like iron that crushes, it shall break and crush all these. And as you saw the feet and toes, partly of potter's clay

and partly of iron, it shall be a divided kingdom, but some of the firmness of iron shall be in it, just as you saw iron mixed with the soft clay. And as the toes of the feet were partly iron and partly clay, so the kingdom shall be partly strong and partly brittle. As you saw the iron mixed with soft clay, so they will mix with one another in marriage, but they will not hold together, just as iron does not mix with clay. And in the days of those kings the God of heaven will set up a kingdom that shall never be destroyed, nor shall the kingdom be left to another people. It shall break in pieces all these kingdoms and bring them to an end, and it shall stand forever, just as you saw that a stone was cut from a mountain by no human hand, and that it broke in pieces the iron, the bronze, the clay, the silver, and the gold. A great God has made known to the king what shall be after this. The dream is certain, and its interpretation sure.

So once again, because God loves people and He devises ways to bring people to him He will give unsaved, non-believers godly dreams. This is a major point in this specific chapter in the Bible. Only God can give interpretations of His dreams. Dreams are mysteries that need to be revealed by God to humanity, as they seek Him.

Daniel chapter 2 verses 27-28:

Daniel answered the king and said, "No wise men, enchanters, magicians, or astrologers can show to the king the mystery that the king has asked, but there is a God in heaven who reveals mysteries, and he has made known to King Nebuchadnezzar what will be in the latter days. Your dream and the visions of your head as you lay in bed are these..."

Chapter Sixteen

❦

Daniel Again

Daniel chapter 7

There is another example of a "dream/vision", in Daniel chapter 7 verse 1:

> In the first year of Belshazzar king of Babylon, Daniel had a dream and visions of the head while he was on his bed. Then he wrote down the dream, telling the main facts.

It would be a marvellous thing to find Daniel's dream journal. There would have been decades and decades of dreams and encounters in the pages. Please note, it is part of Holy Scripture where it clearly tells us while reading this portion of Scripture, that he wrote down the main facts.

This is to insinuate that Daniel didn't get lost in the details. He didn't record everything that he perhaps experienced. I enjoy this part, as I have developed a way for myself when I hear people's dreams, to highlight or capture the main points, and then be able to recognise what God is highlighting to me to share with the dreamer.

We use this Scripture to encourage people to write down their dreams when we train at events, seminars and conferences. We find that a lot of people are not great at memory recall, and we are in jeopardy of losing information that can be important to our lives, should we forget. We want to take every opportunity to give ourselves the best potential of remembering.

We see this in Daniel chapter 2, remember it was the king Nebuchadnezzar who forgot the contents of his dream and was desperate enough to call for people to help him. The point being, we are not good at memory recall. We don't really practice long term memory recall and would have a hard time even at the one week, or most definitely the two-week mark in our past, being able to simply recount details. As the world becomes busier with experiences, advertisements, and information over-load, this point becomes even more applicable to the reader.

Documenting dreams then, is important if you want to be able to refer to your dreams at a later date, as some of the dreams we receive that are from God can be used later in time and not necessarily when we have the dream. A suggestion that I make to people who are interested in documenting their dreams, or placing a value upon them, is to write them down upon waking up and note the time, if a clock is handy; title your dream and date the dream. It is interesting, how many times I have noticed the time after waking from a dream. After I noted the time and documented it, I found it as a passage of Scripture in the Bible. Then the meaning can be applied or confirmed by using the Scripture, due to the time noted. On more regular occasions the time has no significance, other than noting the time or seeing when I get godly dreams given to me.

Let's look at another book in the Bible—Habakkuk chapter 2, verse 1:

> I will take my stand at my watch post and station myself on the tower and look out to see what he will say to me, and what I will answer concerning my complaint.

Habakkuk has removed himself to seek the face of God, to hear what God would tell him. We call this 'going to our secret place' or 'the prayer closet'—it is referred to by many phrases. The thing to see is, that Habakkuk was waiting to hear from God.

Then taking a closer look, we can see in the book of Habakkuk chapter 2 verses 2-3:

> And the Lord answered me, "Write the vision; make it plain on tablets, so he may run who reads it. For still the vision awaits its appointed time; it hastens to the end—it will not lie. If it seems slow, wait for it; it will surely come; it will not delay."

There are many suggestions about how to record or help you as a dreamer, to record your dreams. Having an old-fashioned notepad and pen next to your bed, a journal that is your dream journal, an iPad, iPhone or tablet nearby (perhaps not so close to where you sleep but handy), a small tape device or something you can speak into.

One of the things I would like to mention here is that your dream vocabulary will be different to someone else's. Remember, God wants to give you understanding.

He will use people who you know, and familiar things related to your life, to speak to you. Therefore, you cannot use your aunt, uncle, or relative to help someone else understand their dream. Your dream is custom fit for you, if it is applied to you. So if you have, for instance, a dream about a little black dog and it was the little puppy you got on Christmas morning and it represents the gift you always wanted, let's say; you can not interpret every black dog as positive, if someone else tells you their dream and wants help interpreting. A huge point that I make is, not everyone can interpret another person's dream!

We need to ask the Holy Spirit, and not rely on a resource book or journal. God will highlight things and mention things to us, and when spoken, the person will have peace or, when something just fits inside of the person and they know, yes, that is what that means.

Daniel also had a type of dream which is about the future. Daniel actually saw visions of the future, actual events that would take place, with his eyes wide open:

Daniel chapter 8, verse 3:

> I raised my eyes and saw, and behold, a ram standing on the bank of the canal. It had two horns, and both horns were high, but one was higher than the other, and the higher one came up last.

Daniel chapter 10, verse 7:

> And I, Daniel, alone saw the vision, for the men who were with me did not see the vision, but a

great trembling fell upon them, and they fled to hide themselves.

In this experience that Daniel had, the spiritual realm was opened up to him. God showed him future events that would take place. These were not symbolic of something else happening, but the reality of God's plan was revealed so that the future events would be shared with Daniel. Please note, that even though Daniel could see, others around him could not see, but they definitely experience the fear of God that can accompany encounters. They run away, because, of being overcome by the experience. Then the same truth could be written down and shared with all the readers of Scripture throughout the centuries to follow!

God loves to share His plans and intentions with humanity before they take place. God proves He is God and there is no other.

> For the Lord God does nothing without revealing his secret to his servants the prophets. The lion has roared; who will not fear? The Lord God has spoken; who can but prophesy? (Amos chapter 3 verse 7)

This is a wonderful relationship that God extends to humanity to partake in the plan of God, through prayer and understanding, that God proves over and over again to creation. He alone knows everything, it is what we call 'omniscient'. Time exists in a different way, in the realm that Daniel was able to see into. Some of the events that he saw have still yet to be fulfilled to this day. Therefore, we can ascertain from this that there are no specific timelines that accompany these revelations.

How do we quiet ourselves? Again, there are no right or wrongs when it comes to seeking God to speak to us. The phrase, 'still oneself or quiet yourself', is used in some circles. Mark chapter 1 verse 35 says:

> And rising very early in the morning, while it was still dark, he departed and went out to a desolate place, and there he prayed.

Jesus, as our example, seeks time with his Heavenly Father first. He removes all distraction from his life. This is the key to being able to develop our hearing when God wants to communicate to us. Our technology, as fast and as instant as it becomes, does not replace the fundamental necessity of spending time with God, removed from distractions.

I have found in my own life, when this happens all these thoughts and things I need to do start popping into my mind, are you the same? Well, I take a piece of paper sometimes, and I write down what I think the Lord is instructing me or sharing with me—it is a 'prayer journal', if you want to call it that. Then, I write down on the right-hand margin things that pop into my head to do, or people to call. Whatever it is, write it down and save it for later. The more I'm determined to stay on the course of meeting with God, less and less the ideas, thoughts and the 'to do' list, grow. It is a battle. The mind is where the battle is for most of us.

I just want to give some more Scriptures about taking time out to have quiet time, or 'going to the mountain top', with God:

John chapter 6 verse 15:

Perceiving then that they were about to come and take him by force to make him king, Jesus withdrew again to the mountain by himself.

Luke chapter 22 verses 39-46:

And he came out and went, as was his custom, to the Mount of Olives, and the disciples followed him. And when he came to the place, he said to them, "Pray that you may not enter into temptation." And he withdrew from them about a stone's throw, and knelt down and prayed, saying, "Father, if you are willing, remove this cup from me. Nevertheless, not my will, but yours, be done." And there appeared to him an angel from heaven, strengthening him. And being in agony he prayed more earnestly; and his sweat became like great drops of blood falling down to the ground. And when he rose from prayer, he came to the disciples and found them sleeping for sorrow, and he said to them, "Why are you sleeping? Rise and pray that you may not enter into temptation."

Luke chapter 5 verse 15:

But he would withdraw to desolate places and pray.

Mark chapter 6 verses 46-48:

And after he had taken leave of them, he went up on the mountain to pray. And when evening came, the boat was out on the sea, and he was alone on the land. And he saw that they were making headway painfully, for the wind was against them. And about the fourth watch of the night he came to them, walking on the sea. He meant to pass by them…

Daniel chapter 7 verses 1-8:

> In the first year of Belshazzar king of Babylon, Daniel saw a dream and visions of his head as he lay in his bed. Then he wrote down the dream and told the sum of the matter. Daniel declared, "I saw in my vision by night, and behold, the four winds of heaven were stirring up the great sea. And four great beasts came up out of the sea, different from one another. The first was like a lion and had eagles' wings. Then as I looked its wings were plucked off, and it was lifted up from the ground and made to stand on two feet like a man, and the mind of a man was given to it. And behold, another beast, a second one, like a bear. It was raised up on one side. It had three ribs in its mouth between its teeth; and it was told, 'Arise, devour much flesh.' After this I looked, and behold, another, like a leopard, with four wings of a bird on its back. And the beast had four heads, and dominion was given to it. After this I saw in the night visions, and behold, a fourth beast, terrifying and dreadful and exceedingly strong. It had great iron teeth; it devoured and broke in pieces and stamped what was left with its feet. It was different from all the beasts that were before it, and it had ten horns. I considered the horns, and behold, there came up among them another horn, a little one, before which three of the first horns were plucked up by the roots. And behold, in this horn were eyes like the eyes of a man, and a mouth speaking great things.

Interestingly, in the first verse it says visions, plural form, and 'of his head'. What does this infer? Well, if you compare this with the vision that John had in the book of Revelation, the visions that Daniel has in this chapter are within his mind. However, the vision in the book of Revelation are where John is caught up in the realm of the spirit. Metaphoric language is still used in a lot of visions and of course dreams. The visions that Daniel has in chapter 7 alone, would take a book of insight and depth. The amazing thing with God, even though an interpretation is never promised in Scripture to a receiver of such things, God in his grace and mercy gives the person experiencing the revelation, the understanding. See Daniel chapter 7 verses 15-28:

> As for me, Daniel, my spirit within me was anxious, and the visions of my head alarmed me. I approached one of those who stood there and asked him the truth concerning all this. So, he told me and made known to me the interpretation of the things. "These four great beasts are four kings who shall arise out of the earth. But the saints of the Most High shall receive the kingdom and possess the kingdom forever, forever and ever."

> 'Then I desired to know the truth about the fourth beast, which was different from all the rest, exceedingly terrifying, with its teeth of iron and claws of bronze, and which devoured and broke in pieces and stamped what was left with its feet, and about the ten horns that were on its head, and the other horn that came up and before which three of them fell, the horn that had eyes and a mouth that spoke great things, and that seemed greater than its companions. As I looked, this horn made war with the saints and prevailed over them, until the Ancient of Days came, and judgment was given for the saints of the Most High, and the time came when the saints possessed the kingdom.

113

Thus he said: "As for the fourth beast, there shall be a fourth kingdom on earth, which shall be different from all the kingdoms, and it shall devour the whole earth, and trample it down, and break it to pieces. As for the ten horns, out of this kingdom ten kings shall arise, and another shall arise after them; he shall be different from the former ones, and shall put down three kings.

He shall speak words against the Most High, and shall wear out the saints of the Most High, and shall think to change the times and the law; and they shall be given into his hand for a time, times, and half a time. But the court shall sit in judgment, and his dominion shall be taken away, to be consumed and destroyed to the end. And the kingdom and the dominion and the greatness of the kingdoms under the whole heaven shall be given to the people of the saints of the Most High; his kingdom shall be an everlasting kingdom, and all dominions shall serve and obey him."

"Here is the end of the matter. As for me, Daniel, my thoughts greatly alarmed me, and my colour changed, but I kept the matter in my heart."

Chapter Seventeen

∝

Zacharias had a vision not a dream!

Luke chapter 1 verses 5-23

John the Baptist is a well-known biblical character who was a voice crying in the wilderness for people to repent from their sins and be water baptised. His father was an aged priest in the temple and his mother was Elizabeth, cousin of Mary the mother of Jesus.

Zacharias and Elizabeth were aged enough for the event of a child being born to them to be put into the 'ridiculous and miraculous' category. It says in the passage of Scripture found in Luke chapter 1 verses 5-23, that Elizabeth was barren and advanced in years. It also states that they were a righteous couple who were blameless, and living within the commandments and all the statutes of the Lord.

In the days of Herod, king of Judea, there was a priest named Zechariah, of the division of Abijah. And he had a wife from the daughters of Aaron, and her name was Elizabeth. And they were both righteous before God, walking blamelessly in all the commandments and statutes of the Lord. But they had no child, because Elizabeth was barren, and both were advanced in years.

Now while he was serving as priest before God when his division was on duty, according to the custom of the priesthood, he was chosen by lot to enter the temple of the Lord and burn incense. And the whole multitude of the people were praying outside at the hour of incense. And there appeared to him an angel of the Lord standing on the right side of the altar of incense. And Zechariah was troubled when he saw him, and fear fell upon him. But the angel said to him, "Do not be afraid, Zechariah, for your prayer has been heard, and your wife Elizabeth will bear you a son, and you shall call his name John. And you will have joy and gladness, and many will rejoice at his birth, for he will be great before the Lord. And he must not drink wine or strong drink, and he will be filled with the Holy Spirit, even from his mother's womb. And he will turn many of the children of Israel to the Lord their God, and he will go before him in the spirit and power of Elijah, to turn the hearts of the fathers to the children, and the disobedient to the wisdom of the just, to make ready for the Lord a people prepared."

And Zechariah said to the angel, "How shall I know this? For I am an old man, and my wife is advanced in years." And the angel answered him, "I am Gabriel. I stand in the presence of God, and I was sent to speak to you and to bring you this good news. And behold, you will be silent and unable to speak until the day that these things take place, because you did not believe my words, which will be fulfilled in their time." And the people were waiting for Zechariah, and they were wondering at his delay in the temple. And when he came out, he was unable to speak to them, and they realized that he had seen a vision in the temple. And he kept making signs to them and remained mute. And when his time of service was ended, he went to his home. (Luke chapter 1, verses 5-23)

During a time of prayer when incense was being given up to the Lord in the temple, and there were a lot of people praying outside the temple during this time, an angel of the Lord appears on the right side of the table of incense. This must have been a major event in Zacharias' life! An angelic encounter with a message from God to the priest would not have been a common everyday event.

Incense, in many cases in Scripture, is an illustration of prayer. No doubt there would have been many prayers given up to the Lord from this couple. The angel informs Zacharias that his prayer had been heard by God! In the culture of the day, to be barren was a shameful thing to have to endure. We can remember Hannah's plight and the stigma she had to endure from the culture, and the other woman, Peninnah, in the book of 1 Samuel.

God gives us instruction in life. His desire is that we take His lead in directional matters. The angel gives Zacharias the message he would have a son born to Elizabeth and was to name him John. This was a huge issue for Zacharias, not only was his faith being tested in having a son coming, but also that he would have to go against tradition and name his son a name that wasn't part of the family culture and tradition. God will challenge the norm of humanity and implement His purpose and plan. There are times when God gives us an encounter and the revelation that is given to us goes against our culture, traditions, and opinions on a subject.

The angel delivers this message to the priest from God. The events that Zacharias is told would happen, we read later in Scripture, do take place. The angel Gabriel brings some revelation about how John's life will look and what he will not be able to do; and what impact he will have in his calling and ministry.

> For he will be great before the Lord. And he must not drink wine or strong drink, and he will be filled with the Holy Spirit, even from his mother's womb. And he will turn many of the children of Israel to the Lord their God, and he will go before him in the spirit and power of Elijah, to turn the hearts of the fathers to the children, and the disobedient to the wisdom of the just, to make ready for the Lord a people prepared. (Luke chapter 1 verses 15-17)

Unbelief always has a consequence. In this instance the man who was experiencing the encounter, Zacharias, was technically having a vision. Zacharias was told that, because of his unbelief in what he was being told would happen, he would not be able to speak until the baby boy would be born:

> And the angel answered him, "I am Gabriel. I stand in the presence of God, and I was sent to speak to you and to bring you this good news. And behold, you will

be silent and unable to speak until the day that these things take place, because you did not believe my words, which will be fulfilled in their time." (Luke chapter 1, verses 19-20)

Zacharias comes out of the temple where people are waiting for him, and wondering what the delay was for him to show himself. When he comes out of the temple, he is unable to speak and the people realise that he has had a vision. Zacharias makes signs to them but cannot speak. In verse 23, it says, after he finishes his service (work) he then returns home. He would have had to continue his duties in the temple until finished. The reality of what took place, and his unbelief that he would have a son and name him John, had an immediate consequence.

What is the difference between a vision and a dream? I've heard people try to give an answer by saying that a dream is when a person is sleeping and a vision when a person is awake. I disagree with this explanation. When you look at a dream and vision, both can hold metaphoric language or symbols. However, dreams tend to be an illustrative language that needs interpretation, for the symbols used in a dream to represent something else. Visions tend to be literal; by looking at the book of Revelation we can see that it is literal and doesn't represent something else, or hidden meanings.

In this vision that Zechariah has in the book of Luke, it shows that God uses both visions and dreams to communicate His heart. Zechariah needed an 'opinion adjustment'. God chose to use an encounter to change the way Zechariah viewed the world. He had unbelief in his heart and perhaps would not have listened to any other way, except to have his own encounter as a point of reference, and name his son that God chose.

Chapter Eighteen

❧

Joseph

Matthew chapter 1 verse 20
& Matthew chapter 2 verses 13–23

J oseph is the second person with the same name. This Joseph was the betrothed of Mary the mother of Jesus. This Scripture is found in Matthew chapter 1 verses 19-21 (NKJV):

> Then Joseph her husband, being a just man, and not willing to make her a public example, was minded putting her away privily. But while he thought on these things, behold an angel of the Lord appeared unto him in a dream, saying, Joseph, thou son of David, fear not to take unto thee Mary thy wife: for that which is conceived in her is of the Holy Ghost. And she shall bring forth a son, and thou shall call his name Jesus: for he shall save his people from their sins.

Joseph was in serious doubt, and was thinking he would

stop the engagement he found himself in with Mary, because she was pregnant. He is called a just man, a good man according to Scripture; this being God's perspective not humanity's verdict. God gives Joseph a dream to convince the dreamer of the direction and action he should take in his decision making. We read later, that Joseph believed this dream must have been directional from an angel of the Lord because he obeys what he was told to do.

Therefore, dreams that are from the Lord can, once again, be directional. This was one of the greatest decisions of Joseph's life! God intervenes with His plan and makes it very clear what is going on, in detail. Joseph is even told this is a miraculous pregnancy the Holy Ghost has caused to happen to Mary. This has to happen, we read in verse twenty-two of the same chapter, to fulfil Isaiah chapter 7 verse 14:

> Therefore the Lord himself shall give you a sign; Behold, a virgin shall conceive and bear a son, and shall call his name Immanuel.

The statement in Matthew chapter 1 verse 20, 'fear not to take unto Mary thy wife' in the King James Version, in today's English it means, Joseph was afraid to take Mary as his wife because he was, naturally or logically, thinking she had cheated on him with another man. God can use a dream to dispel the fears that hold us back from doing what God wants us to accomplish in life. Fear is one of the tactics and strategies that the enemy of our lives, the Devil, uses to keep us from fulfilling the plan of God for our lives. Even though logical, (and most in Joseph's situation would be thinking the same), through the love of God for all involved and to see God's plan fulfilled, God uses a dream to get the message to Joseph.

Then Joseph has a second dream that has serious significance not only for himself, but also for Mary and Jesus!

Matthew chapter 2 verses 13-15, (KJV):

> And when they were departed, behold, the angel of the Lord appeareth to Joseph in a dream, saying, Arise, and take the young child and his mother, and flee into Egypt, and be thou there until I bring thee word: for Herod will seek the young child to destroy him.
>
> When he arose, he took the young child and his mother by night and departed into Egypt.
>
> And was there until the death of Herod: that it might be fulfilled which was spoken of the Lord by the prophet, saying, Out of Egypt have I called my son.

The scenario found in this portion of Scripture, once again, is to fulfil prophecy spoken over Jesus' life by the prophet, this time Hosea: 'When Israel was a child, I loved him, and out of Egypt I called my son' (Hosea chapter 11, verse 1 NIV).

This is a clear and straight case of a warning dream. Joseph is warned by God in a dream, with the use of an angelic encounter within the dream and directs Joseph to run away to Egypt until he is contacted again. Here Joseph is required to obey, over and over. It is documented to encourage us in the day we currently live. Something so small in Scripture, but the ramifications if Joseph didn't listen could have been cataclysmic! Obedience is really worship to God.

Interestingly, we are told by traditions at Christmas time especially, that the Magi came to visit Jesus in Bethlehem; however, I've asserted that the Magi came and found Jesus when He was a toddler and when He was in Nazareth. If they had been at Bethlehem the family would not have gone to Nazareth to live, before going to Egypt, as it says in Luke chapter 2 verses 39-40 (KJV):

> And when they had performed all things according to the law of the Lord, they returned into Galilee, to their own city Nazareth.
>
> And the child grew and waxed strong in spirit, filled with wisdom: and the grace of God was upon him.

Again, as a side note using Scripture as our point of reference, there are no Scriptures that state the Magi went to Bethlehem, immediately after the birth of Jesus, or that the star the Magi followed led them to a manger.

Then Joseph has a third dream! The third dream is found in Matthew chapter 2 verses 19-21. Remembering that God instructed Joseph to stay in Egypt until further instructed by God, let us look at the passage:

> But when Herod was dead, behold, an angel of the Lord appeareth in a dream to Joseph in Egypt,
>
> Saying, Arise, and take the young child and his mother, and go into the land of Israel: for they are dead which sought the young child's life.

And he arose, and took the young child and his mother, and came into the land of Israel. (KJV)

I love how this encounter proves God's faithfulness! God did what He said He would, and what only He could do. I also want to point out, Joseph was an obedient faith-filled man, to be one who obeyed the instruction to go to Egypt, and then to obey the instruction to go to Israel. Joseph's obedience to God's commands proves he was a man of godly character and devoted to God.

I want to also make another point using this portion of Scripture, where we see the fourth dream of Joseph, continued in Matthew chapter 2 verses 22-23:

But when he heard that Archelaus did reign in Judaea in the room of his father Herod, he was afraid to go thither, notwithstanding, being warned of God in a dream, he turned aside into the parts of Galilee:

And he came and dwelt in a city called Nazareth: that it might be fulfilled which was spoken by the prophets, He shall be called a Nazarene.

Again, Joseph was afraid of Herod's son, who now ruled upon his return to Israel. So God, in His graciousness to Joseph gave him another dream. Joseph has a pure warning dream from God to turn aside from where he might go and instead travel to Galilee. God loves us so much that He will warn us in a dream!

Notice that this was done to fulfil the spoken word from a prophet, and God counted it as from the Holy Spirit so that it would be fulfilled. The prophetic word was not written but spoken. Some are in the habit of saying, only the logos word of God is the way God speaks to humanity, which is true, but here, we see a Rhema word given to the prophet of God in Scripture from the living Spirit of God Himself, which became fulfilled prophecy recorded in Scripture in these two wonderful verses!

Chapter Nineteen

✢

Magi

Matthew chapter 2
verse 12

The Magi are surrounded with mystery and are a part of Scripture that is shrouded in obscurity. Tradition has become a picture, of kings travelling from faraway lands to pay homage to the King of Kings. However, they were astronomers and followed a star or comet, to find the King of Kings, Jesus Christ. It has been depicted to be three men carrying each a gift, but Scripture does not give us an exact number. Gold, Frankincense, and Myrrh were gifts given to Christ from the Magi, but it does not necessarily mean three distinct individuals placed them before Christ.

All that said, they did receive a dream. This is a short account and, because it is so short, perhaps some readers might glance over this Scripture and miss a valid point about dreams, that God can give to us. The dream they received was definitely, a warning or directional dream. If you remember, Herod in verse 7 of Matthew chapter 2, spoke to the 'wise men' (as they are referred to privately). He was diligent about asking when or at what time they saw the star? Herod, in verse eight, sends them to Bethlehem and tells the 'wise men' to send a message to Herod when they find the child, so he also could worship the child.

> Then Herod summoned the wise men secretly and ascertained from them what time the star had appeared. And he sent them to Bethlehem, saying, "Go and search diligently for the child, and when you have found him, bring me word, that I too may come and worship him." (Matthew chapter 2, verses 7-8)

Let's look at the base Scripture and reference to the dream that the Magi received:

> And when they were come into the house they saw the young child with Mary his mother, and fell down, and worshipped him: and when they had opened their treasures, they presented unto him gifts, gold, and frankincense, and myrrh. And being warned of God in a dream that they should not return to Herod, they departed into their own country another way. (Matthew chapter 2 verses 11-12)

It doesn't name who had the dream, interestingly it does attribute the Magi or 'wise men' of having a godly dream, as it says, 'they'. Here it is written in plural form, for more than one. We learn in the New Testament Scriptures, that a dream can be for more than one person to benefit from. God wants to speak to individuals through relationship which, to refer to the previous portions of

Scripture, Joseph in my opinion, had a relationship with God. He was an important figure in the life of Christ, being a surrogate father on earth, so to speak, for Jesus. Joseph was in Jesus' life, most assuredly, until Jesus was 12, because Mary and Joseph found Him in the temple together when He went missing, see Luke chapter 2 verses 42-51:

> And when he was twelve years old, they went up according to custom. And when the feast was ended, as they were returning, the boy Jesus stayed behind in Jerusalem. His parents did not know it, but supposing him to be in the group they went a day's journey, but then they began to search for him among their relatives and acquaintances, and when they did not find him, they returned to Jerusalem, searching for him. After three days they found him in the temple, sitting among the teachers, listening to them and asking them questions. And all who heard him were amazed at his understanding and his answers. And when his parents saw him, they were astonished. And his mother said to him, "Son, why have you treated us so? Behold, your father and I have been searching for you in great distress." And he said to them, "Why were you looking for me? Did you not know that I must be in my Father's house?" And they did not understand the saying that he spoke to them. And he went down with them and came to Nazareth and was submissive to them. And his mother treasured up all these things in her heart.

The point of the Magi is, that the dream was for more than one person. The warning given was for the Magi, plurally. There are times when the plan of God encompasses more than one person to obey and be a part of the plan. God intended to keep the Magi safe, as well as Jesus safe, from the evil plan of Herod to kill Jesus and thus allowing the plan of Satan to win.

I think it is interesting to note again, that the word for child in the original Greek is, 'pais', which is a child that is older than a "brephos," a newly born infant baby, which is the word used when the shepherds were found over a year before at Jesus' birth; see Luke chapter 2, verse 16: 'And they went with haste and found Mary and Joseph, and the baby lying in a manger.'

The point I want to emphasise with the Magi is, for the purpose of warning them, the dream was for the group, of 'wise men'. God didn't want them to help Herod or contact him. The Magi were directed by God not to return to Herod.

Matthew chapter 2, verse 16 says:

> Then Herod, when he saw that he was mocked of the wise men, was exceedingly angry, and sent forth, and slew all the children that were in Bethlehem, and in all of the coasts thereof, from two years old and under, according to the time which he had diligently enquired of the wise men.

This, once again, is fulfilled prophecy through the prophet Jeremiah:

> Thus, says the Lord: "A voice is heard in Ramah, lamentation and bitter weeping. Rachel is weeping for her children; she refuses to be comforted for her children, because they are no more". (Jeremiah

chapter 31, verse 15)

God does use dreams to communicate His desire to more than one person connected to His purpose and plans. Dreams and visions are not the only way of communication. God loves to use many parts to make a whole. He is weaving a huge mosaic over centuries and millennia. He uses many parts, working together and in different circumstances, to produce life and the maintaining of that life. This is what I like to compare dream interpretation to; like a massive jigsaw puzzle or colouring box of crayons, trying to get a frame to work with, or an outline to fill in with colour and expression of meaning.

First and foremost, ask the Holy spirit to give you, the dreamer, insight. It's written in Scripture that we don't have because we, simply, don't ask. I find that I need to be reminded of things over and over. Finally, the penny drops so to speak, and understanding comes either through repetition or maturity in my life. Faith is always required. James chapter 4 verse 2: 'You do not have, because you do not ask'.

Chapter Twenty

∂℃

Pilate's Wife

Matthew chapter 27
verse 19

This is the last official mention of a dreamer recorded in Scripture: It is Pilate's wife who, we can read, has a disturbing dream and it is during the crucial point, in the account, where Pilate is weighing a decision of who would be released; either Jesus or Barabbas, as it was the governor's custom at the feast to release to the crowd a prisoner of their choosing.

> Now at the feast the governor was accustomed to release for the crowd any one prisoner whom they wanted. (Matthew chapter 27, verse 15)

Pilate was the Roman representative. Scripture clearly states that Pilate knew that the Jews had handed Jesus over to him because of envy. Matthew chapter 27, verse 18:

> For he knew that it was out of envy that they had
> delivered him up.

At this crucial moment in history, and while Pilate is sitting in the place called the judgement seat, his wife sends him a message.

> Have nothing to do with that innocent man, for I have
> suffered terribly in a dream today because of Him.
> (Matthew chapter 27 verse 19)

I mention this very obscure verse, as it is so interesting to me, that God would choose once again to use a dream to interject truth in the most crucial moment in history! God's plan is underway, the plan to eradicate the power of sin over humanity, once and for all, through the death and resurrection of Christ. God chooses to give a dream in this vital point in the story.

Pilate was not a follower of Jesus nor was his wife, by any indication in the Bible, historical writings, or accounts outside of Scripture. Yet Pilate, from Scripture, knew that Jesus was an innocent man. He even washes his hands with water, as a prophetic symbol that he is innocent of the Jewish leaders and people's request to crucify Jesus. When God could use any form or means to state the truth, and give Pilate opportunity to release Jesus, God the Father chooses a dream at that moment in time.

Pilate's wife even calls Jesus innocent; they might have had a conversation earlier about Jesus. Jesus was that popular and His ministry would have reached conversations around the area. However, she says that she has suffered terribly in the dream. That is an important and emphatic statement! I believe the dream she received told her that Jesus was innocent. She must have been so affected by the content of the dream, she knew she had to get the message to Pilate. By that message, which was truth, Pilate was without excuse!

Have you ever wondered about this whole set up by the Father God toward the Son Jesus Christ? If you take a look at Scripture, there are so many prophecies that state clearly that Jesus would be crucified. The detail of Jesus' life before His physical birth is truly amazing and can only be explained through the plan of God. So, why would God allow a dream to be given once again, to a non-follower of Christ when, the result was assuredly desired by the Creator of everything, to be a result of death for the Son of God?

God always gives humanity opportunity to receive the truth. The word used for the English word *dream* in Matthew chapter 27 verse 19, is only used six times in Scripture. Every other time in Scripture is when Jesus is a baby and child. It is fascinating to me, that God even uses a word that means *dream* but is cloaked in obscurity. God loves to hide truth and revelation.

> It is the glory of God to hide truth and the glory of a
> king to search the hidden thing out. (Proverbs chapter
> 25 verse 2 KJV)

I want to reiterate the subject of God hiding things and men searching the meaning out. This could be very frustrating for people to find that it is, actually, a pattern with the way God does things. In Psalm chapter 78, verse 2, God used the psalmist to give us a prophetic insight into the way God would have Jesus communicate: God chose for Jesus to use parabolic language.

> I will open my mouth in a parable; I will utter dark sayings from of old… (Psalm chapter 78, verse 2 KJV)

This, in fact, becomes a problem to the disciples in Matthew chapter 13, verses 10-13:

> Then the disciples came and said to him, "Why do you speak to them in parables?" And he answered them, "To you it has been given to know the secrets of the kingdom of heaven, but to them it has not been given. For to the one who has, more will be given, and he will have an abundance, but from the one who has not, even what he has will be taken away. This is why I speak to them in parables, because seeing they do not see, and hearing they do not hear, nor do they understand."

Hard sayings or riddles are also used in Scripture. It is where God wants to build curiosity in our lives to search out the meaning.

God spoke with Moses differently than he did with others, as we see in Numbers chapter 1, verse 8: 'With him I speak mouth to mouth, clearly, and not in riddles, and he beholds the form of the Lord. Why then were you not afraid to speak against my servant Moses?'

When we look in a Bible concordance, like the 'Strong's Concordance' and look up the original Hebrew word used for dark saying, it is *chiydah*, meaning, 'parable' or 'dark saying', 'riddle', 'perplexing question' or 'double meaning'.

The prophet Ezekiel was commanded by God to put a riddle forward to the nation of Israel in the book of Ezekiel, chapter 17, verse 2: 'Son of man, put forth a riddle, and speak a parable unto the house of Israel'.

In the book of Ecclesiastes chapter 5, verse 7, I'm paraphrasing, but through the words of Solomon I interpret it as saying, not to base life just upon dreams; and I'm certainly not advocating such a lifestyle: "No matter how much you dream, how much useless work you do, or how much you talk, you must still stand in awe of God".

I want to rely on every word that proceeds out of the mouth of God and develop life skills, relationship exercises and skills, to do just that. Matthew chapter 4 verse 4: "Man shall not live by bread alone, but by every word that comes from the mouth of God".

The Greek word used for 'comes from' (and other translations use 'proceeds'), is the word *Ekporeuomai*. This word depicts the picture of a river flowing out of the mouth of God. The Greek word for mouth in this Scripture, is the word, *Stoma*. This word is like the edge of a sword.

As I've previously stated, God wants to communicate to people out of love and a heart of wanting relationship with his creation. God communicates from His heart toward our heart. He will use anything to communicate His intent. In my opinion, He even uses the wife of a Roman official to speak truth in a hidden Scripture, in the most wonderful and impacting true story ever recounted—the death of Jesus Christ and eventual resurrection, and soon coming return!

Chapter Twenty-One

❦

Jesus
—what?

Jesus? Are you telling me Jesus interpreted dreams? Where is the Scripture for that? Well, it is a funny thing! We actually have to dig a little deeper in our last chapter to find the answers to this very good group of questions. You might have been told, as was I, that the only dream interpreters in Scripture were Joseph and Daniel. However, when you look a little closer in Scripture, we can see by a mere definition of a word that is applied to Jesus, whereby we come up with a slightly different and interesting picture.

Have you ever looked at Scripture and wondered if there's more to that verse than meets the eye? I'm not talking about deleting and adding to Scripture, I'm talking about digging for gold in Scripture to get to 'the meat' of the Word!

In Psalm chapter 78 verse 2, is a prophetic word, foretelling that Jesus would speak in parabolic language or, what some call, dark speech. Now, dark speech has nothing to do with darkness associated with evil. What dark speech means, is that, it is a riddle or mysterious in nature and not easily understood, without the understanding that can only come from the Holy Spirit. The word used in the Hebrew language is the word, *Chiyodah,* which means riddle, puzzle or dark saying, a hard saying, hard question or parable. Jesus definitely told parables, which I mentioned in the previous chapter, to the point it drives the disciples to ask the Messiah, why do you talk like this? (see Matthew chapter 13 verses 10-13)

The way Jesus spoke puzzled the disciples, to the point of asking Jesus. Yes, they asked Jesus… why do you speak the way you do? They didn't make a connection with regard to Psalm chapter 78, verse 2 in regard to the Messiah's speech. They were not unlike us today, where we don't understand sometimes how and why God is communicating to us a certain thing, or why He is doing something or allowing something, in a certain way.

Isaiah chapter 55 verses 8-9 (NKJV):

"For My thoughts are not your thoughts, nor are your ways My ways," says the Lord. "For as the heavens are higher than the earth, So, are My ways higher than your ways, And My thoughts than your thoughts."

It clearly says about Jesus, "and Jesus increased in wisdom and stature, and in favour with God and men", see Luke chapter 2 verse 52. We have to look at the definition in the passage, to come up with an understanding of what was going on in Jesus that He was increasing in.

The word *stature* is about Him growing up physically and maturing into a man. The word *wisdom* is a more interesting word, in regard to the area of dreams and even visions. If you were to go to a biblical dictionary, or look up in a concordance, like Strong's, to see what it says about the word wisdom (which is the word *Sophia* in the Greek language), a person would come up with this definition: 'wisdom, broad and full of intelligence; used of the knowledge of very diverse matters'.

Remember, this exact word is attached to the life of Jesus! He created seven spirits of God, found in Isaiah chapter 11 verses 2-3:

> And the Spirit of the Lord shall rest upon him, the Spirit of wisdom and understanding, the Spirit of counsel and might, the Spirit of knowledge and the fear of the Lord. And his delight shall be in the fear of the Lord. He shall not judge by what his eyes see, or decide disputes by what his ears hear.

He created humanity with the ability to have wisdom as a part of life on earth. Remember Solomon who prayed for wisdom to be his and it was granted? Jesus, the Son of Man and the Son of God, and the wisdom which belongs to men, has several areas attached to it. Jesus would have had each of these in which He was increasing in as He grew older and then became Rabbi, teacher. Jesus would have had very specific and diverse knowledge of things human, and that which pertains to God, or the Divine. Wisdom is acquired by learning and experience. You can read about His wisdom by looking at the parables, especially in Matthew chapter 13.

Jesus would have been able to use the act of

interpreting dreams and always giving sound advice. How can we say that? When you look up the definition of wisdom in the original Greek you will see this is clearly one of the definitions of the word. This is actually one of the definitions found in most biblical lexicons for the meaning of wisdom, *Sophia*.

The definition goes on to include the intelligence that is seen in discovering the meaning of some mysterious number or vision. Again, Jesus is described as growing in wisdom in Scripture, in Luke chapter 2, verse 52. The definition of this word includes the meaning applied to Jesus, as being able to know the meaning of mysterious numbers or a vision.

Therefore, in answer to the question, there are no Scriptures, as such, to point out Jesus had interpreted a specific person's dream or, had a dream from the Father God. However, by the definition of the word wisdom, Jesus would have been able to interpret dreams and visions that were given to Himself, or others!

Jesus, being totally God, is the one that designed dreams and visions to be a form of communicating to humanity, when He was creating everything that is seen and unseen. As I try to tell people—to have a dream, God came up with it first! God is the giver of dreams and He thought of the imagery and the content first, in order to deliver it to people. The dreams that Pharaoh and Pilate's wife had were not first experienced by them, in their minds or being, but it was created and delivered by the Divine, by God!

God has callings, healings, deliverance and inventions for humanity. It all came from Him and is delivered to the dreamer, the recipient of the imagery, in picture language. God is the one who designed us with all sorts of gifting, capacity and abilities. He designed humanity to be interactive. He created us to communicate His heart and intentions for us. How extraordinary is this all-knowing, all-powerful, ever-existent, eternal, everywhere-at-the-same-time, God!

If you have never had a dream from God and you want to have one, ask Him for one! God has a funny way of giving us His desire and covering it with the wrapping paper of our desire. Some of us shut down dreaming because of nightmares and night trauma experienced when we were small, or even as an adult. Ask God to heal you from the effects of that; and ask Him to give you a godly dream. Perhaps you want to show God, 'Hey I'm serious about this', and you can get a notepad or journal and a pen and place them near where you sleep. Maybe you want to record it on your phone, so you can press play, then use that to take notes in some way, later.

There will be a lot of people who will go to heaven knowing the forgiveness and love of Jesus, and never remember a dream. Having a dream is not a pre-requisite to going to heaven. Thank God, I say! However, you may be a person who wants to enjoy what God might want to allow you to experience. A dream or a vision from Him may be the very thing He wants to use, to allow for you to get to know Him better! I'll leave you with this as I close this book—one of my absolute favourite Scriptures:

> That the God of our Lord Jesus Christ, the Father of glory, may give to you the spirit of wisdom and revelation in the knowledge of Him, the eyes of your understanding being enlightened; that you may know

what the hope of His calling is, what are the riches of the glory of His inheritance in the saints. (Ephesians chapter 1, verses 17-18 NKJV)

Some translations read 'that you may know Him better'. My encouragement is that anything God has for us is so we know Him better through extended relationship, and not just to have a spiritual experience. Remember God first loved us! 1 John chapter 4, verse 9:

We love Him because He first loved us.

The Scriptures also say, man cannot come to God unless God draws us to Himself, see John chapter 6 verse 44 (NIV):

No one can come to me unless the Father who sent me draws him. And I will raise him up on the last day.

My prayer is, that you will be more open to allowing God to bring you into a deeper place of awe and wonder of Him. That, we would all be more receptive to God revealing Himself and to know Him better. This *could* take place through a dream or a vision but does not *need* to be the way He engages us.

My continued prayer is, that when we look into Scripture, and I encourage every believer to continue to pursue reading the Scripture daily, we gain understanding more and more, into this beautiful relationship available to us all. This amazing only true God, Jesus Christ, the Giver of His Dreams!

Chapter Twenty-Two

⁓

Encouraging You

God still speaks to us in many forms just as he did in biblical times. Hebrews chapter 13 verse 8 tells us that 'Jesus Christ is the same yesterday and today and forever', therefore, he still chooses to communicate through dreams, just as he did in the past. He is personal and individual, longing to speak with us in ways we understand, and if that, for you, is through dreams, then take note, and take the time to seek to understand the wonderful things he is saying. How special it is that he wants a close personal relationship with us.

I want to encourage every reader to, at the very least, be open to the truth that God does give dreams today for the benefit of humanity. I do not have dreams every single night or even on a regular basis. I have had the wonderful ability by the Holy Spirit to help people interpret what God might be saying to the dreamer. This does not make me an expert and I make no such claim. I have tried to study and research through Scripture, and relationally from people of diverse cultures where dreams are a part of the accepted way that God speaks to people.

Not every dream or experience that seems dream-like is a pleasant experience, even when initiated by God. In chapter 4 of the book of Job, Eliphaz has an experience we read about, in verses 12 to 21:

> Now a word was brought to me stealthily;
> my ear received the whisper of it.
> Amid thoughts from visions of the night,
> when deep sleep falls on men,
> dread came upon me, and trembling,
> which made all my bones shake.
> A spirit glided past my face;
> the hair of my flesh stood up.
> It stood still,
> but I could not discern its appearance.
> A form was before my eyes;
> there was silence, then I heard a voice:
> "Can mortal man be in the right before God?
> Can a man be pure before his Maker?
> Even in his servants he puts no trust,
> and his angels he charges with error;
> how much more those who dwell in houses of clay,
> whose foundation is in the dust,
> who are crushed like the moth.
> Between morning and evening they are beaten to pieces;
> they perish forever without anyone regarding it.
> Is not their tent-cord plucked up within them,
> do they not die, and that without wisdom?"

In this portion of Scripture, we see that God wanted to

make a very distinctive point, that He is God, and in doing this he allows the fear of the Lord to accompany the experience, as to make the point pronounced.

God also wants to use visions and dreams throughout the generations and, it seems, throughout one's personal growth, chapter 2 of the book of Joel verses 28 and 29:

> And it shall come to pass afterward,
> that I will pour out my Spirit on all flesh;
> your sons and your daughters shall prophesy,
> your old men shall dream dreams,
> and your young men shall see visions.
> Even on the male and female servants
> in those days I will pour out my Spirit.

Notice, in this chapter of Scripture, old men shall dream dreams, and young men shall see visions. I love how God has a plan for the young and the aged. This also shows the plan of God, as He wants male and female servants to experience the Holy Spirit being poured out. God loves all of humanity. Jesus Christ came to earth in the form of a man, while still being totally man and totally God. It is a mystery to people of how this could be so, yet, it is truth according to the Word of God.

God uses the Bible, prayer, prophesy and words of knowledge, wisdom and teaching of Scripture, as well as dreams and visions, to communicate His heart and intent to our hearts and minds. So many things today, can be used to be divisive by the enemy of our souls. God never intended for people to use gifting and abilities, that He can only deliver to a person's life, as being allowed to become a tool of a fake caste system. 'God does not have

147

grandchildren' is an appropriate saying. God only has His children, and they are those who make the choice to become His children, by accepting the Lord Jesus Christ as their personal Saviour, asking Jesus to forgive them of their sins and asking Him to rule and reign in their heart and life.

What I mean by this is, God, throughout Scripture, shows Himself as real. He doesn't just pick one nation or people group to be His one and only. Read the book of Romans, chapters 9, 10 and 11. How wonderful a plan, that God's grace was extended to, not only the Jewish people, but to the whole of humanity. A dream can be used by God to get the attention of Pilate's wife, and yet also to get to the Pharaoh, ruler of the known world. He can give an accurate dream, with a God-given revelation inside of the dream, to your enemy, as He did Gideon with the Midianite soldier. God is fascinating, wonderful, marvellous, incredible, and to think that the God of the entirety of everything created, seen and unseen, wants to communicate to a person, is overwhelmingly cool.

This God, who allows himself to be revealed and experienced through Jesus Christ, and the truth found in the pages of Scripture, invented the entire concept of dreams for His purpose and pleasure. The book of Psalms, chapter 115, verse 3:

> Our God is in the heavens;
> he does all that he pleases.

The book of Job chapter 42, verse 2:

> I know that you can do all things,
> and that no purpose of yours can be thwarted.

The book of Proverbs chapter 16, verse 9:

> The heart of man plans his way,
> but the Lord establishes his steps.

The book of Hebrews chapter 1, verse 3:

> He is the radiance of the glory of God and the exact
> imprint of his nature, and he upholds the universe by
> the word of his power. After making purification for
> sins, he sat down at the right hand of the Majesty on
> high.

So, why place these Scriptures within this chapter? God
is Sovereign and in total power and has all Authority. He
has given the amazing gift of free will. It is my opinion,
that most people in the Western culture, have an opinion
of a conditioning to say that, something must be one
thing or the other. It is either this or it is that. However, it
is my opinion that in most cases it is both. God is totally
Sovereign, yet He allows man to make choices within his
Sovereign reign over life on earth. Meanwhile, God can
override man's will if He so chooses.

What does this have to do with dreams? Well, a
person can dismiss the truth that God does use dreams
today. He or she can decide to not believe that God would
even use a dream.

Take a look at the book of Job chapter 33 and
verses 12 through 18:

> Behold, in this you are not right. I will answer you,
> for God is greater than man.
> Why do you contend against him,

saying, 'He will answer none of man's words'?
For God speaks in one way,
and in two, though man does not perceive it.
In a dream, in a vision of the night,
when deep sleep falls on men,
while they slumber on their beds,
then he opens the ears of men
and terrifies them with warnings,
that he may turn man aside from his deed
and conceal pride from a man;
he keeps back his soul from the pit,
his life from perishing by the sword.

These Scriptures show, that God gave free will to humanity, and there are many more than what I am referring to in this chapter. The book of Galatians chapter 5 verse 13, 16-17:

For you were called to freedom, brothers. Only do not use your freedom as an opportunity for the flesh, but through love serve one another.

But I say, walk by the Spirit, and you will not gratify the desires of the flesh. For the desires of the flesh are against the Spirit, and the desires of the Spirit are against the flesh, for these are opposed to each other, to keep you from doing the things you want to do.

The book of Mark chapter 8 and verse 34:

And calling the crowd to him with his disciples, he said to them, "If anyone would come after me, let him deny himself and take up his cross and follow me.

The book of Philippians chapter 2 and verses 12-13:

> Therefore, my beloved, as you have always obeyed, so now, not only as in my presence but much more in my absence, work out your own salvation with fear and trembling, for it is God who works in you, both to will and to work for his good pleasure.

My hope is that you would read this book and be more open to God, perhaps, giving you a dream someday for His purpose. That we all would be open to God speaking to humanity, and if not, our self, then may we be more open to allowing that to take place in someone else's life. We have a life to be lived on earth that is exciting, and worth the daily choice to pursue God in relationship, only through Jesus Christ and the power of the Holy Spirit. God has given us the Bible, a book to live our life by its standard and Truth. We have taken a look at the dreams found in Scripture, and I pray that, as you read the pages of the Bible and go after Him with a whole heart, you will find His communication for yourself. May you now be stirred to receive God-inspired dreams.

Notes

1. Morton T Kelsey, *God Dreams and Revelation* (Augsburg Fortress Minneapolis, 1974), 9.

2. Freud S, *The Interpretation of Dreams*, the Standard Edition of the Complete Works of Sigmund Freud, vols 4,5 (Ed J Strachey London; Hogarth Press, 1900)

3. Morton T Kelsey, *God Dreams and Revelation* (Augsburg Fortress Minneapolis, 1974), 172 &186

4. C.G. Jung, *Collected Works*, vol 5 (New York; Random House [Pantheon Books], 1956), 16ff.

5. McLeod, S. A. (2018, May 21). *Carl Jung*. Simply Psychology. https://www.simplypsychology.org/carl-jung. html

6. Hank O'Mahoney, "Becoming the Dream - A Gestalt Approach" *Inside Out*. Irish Association of Humanistic and Integrative Psychotherapy. IAHIP: *https://iahip.org/inside-out/issue-12-spring-1993/becoming-the-dream-a-gestalt-approach* (Issue 12: Spring 1993)

7. Josie Malenowski, "Was Freud Right About Dreams After

All?" *The conversation*, http://theconversation.com/was-freud-right-about-dreams-after-all-heres-the-research-that-helps-explain-it-60884 (July 14, 2016).

8. Eugene Aserinsky, Nathaniel Kleitman, "Regularly Occurring Periods of Eye Motility and Concomitant Phenomena, During Sleep," *AAAS Science* Vol. 118, Issue 3062, (04 September, 1953), pp.273-274.

9. Michelle Carr PhD, "A Brief History of Dream Research" *Psychology Today, Dream Factory, https://www. psychologytoday.com/au/blog/dream-factory/201606/brief-history-dream-research* (June 30th, 2016).

10. Hobson, J.A & McCarley, R. "The brain as a dream state generator: An activation-synthesis hypothesis of the dream process". *American journal of Psychiatry* 134, (1977) 1335-1348

11. John Pratt Bingham, *God and Dreams: Is There a Connection?* Page 44, www.books.google.com.au copyright 2010 Wipf and Stock publishers, Eugene, Oregon USA

12. Morton T. Kelsey, *God Dreams and Revelation: A Christian Interpretation of Dreams,* (Augsburg Fortress Minneapolis, 1974), 70.

13. James W. Goll, Michal Ann Goll, *Dream Language: The Prophetic Power of Dreams*, (Destiny Image Publishers, 2006), 57.

14. Institute for Spiritual Development Level 201 notes Prophetic history page 6, 2004 version.

15. Morton T. Kelsey, *God Dreams, and Revelation: A*

Christian Interpretation of Dreams, (Augsburg Fortress Minneapolis, 1974), 107.

[16.] Morton T. Kelsey, *God Dreams, and Revelation: A Christian Interpretation of Dreams*, (Augsburg Fortress Minneapolis, 1974), 105.

[17.] Morton T. Kelsey, *God Dreams, and Revelation: A Christian Interpretation of Dreams*, (Augsburg Fortress Minneapolis, 1974), 106.

[18.] Franz Rosenthal, Journal of the American Oriental Society Vol.85, No.2 (Apr.–June., 1965), pp. 139-144 Published by: American Oriental Society DOI:10.2307/597984 https://www.jstor.org/stable/597984

You can connect with David Fenton at:

email: mountaincollective19@gmail.com
https://mountaincollective.org.au/

https://www.facebook.com/mountaincollective.org.au/

https://www.instagram.com/mountain__collective/

CPSIA information can be obtained
at www.ICGtesting.com
Printed in the USA
LVHW090734270720
661544LV00013B/192

9 780648 460220